THE COMPLETE BOOK OF

Children's PARTIES

CLARE BEATON

CONTENTS

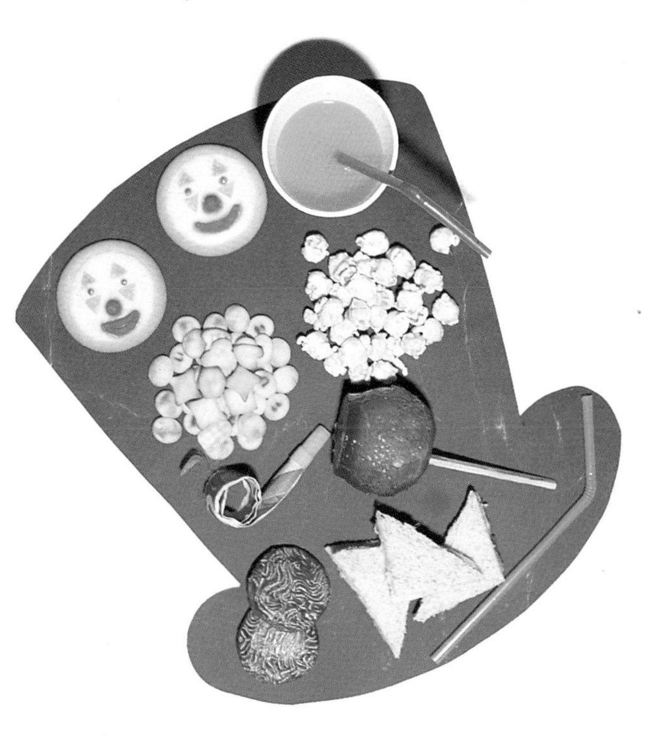

Kingfisher Books
NEW YORK

1 · THEMES

INTRODUCTION

Having a party theme adds greatly to the fun and excitement and encourages children to join in and use their imaginations.

This section is full of ideas and useful tips, including suggestions for sending invitations, creating decorations, choosing costumes, food, games, and party favors.

Remember to tailor the party to the children attending. Very young children do not enjoy games with complicated rules. In general, keep games simple and vary the pace with quiet games, alternating them with more boisterous activity. Parties involving different age groups and mixes of boys and girls need careful planning. However much you may wish otherwise, boys and girls may have different ideas about what they want to wear, eat, and play.

A theme party doesn't require extra work on your part, just some planning ahead. For example, much of the food can be made in advance and then kept in the freezer or in airtight containers. Children love music, so choose some records or tapes for them to sing and dance to. Try and enlist some extra adult help on the day of the party to ensure everything goes smoothly.

PREPARATION 1

Invitations

This book gives you ideas to help you make party invitations. Why not get the birthday child to help you? This will give you both a fun activity to share.

If you are going to use envelopes, remember to measure them first, so you can make the invitations to fit.

Give invitations out about two weeks before the day of the party – early enough to avoid disappointment on refusal, but not so early that the date gets forgotten!

Make your invitations from brightly colored paper or cardboard. Keep illustrations simple and uncluttered. If you have access to a photocopying machine you can simply make copies of a drawing, stick them on colored paper and color them in.

Collage art is also fun, easy to do, and very effective. Cut or tear up old magazines or comics and stick the pictures on cardboard. Differently sized lettering from old newspapers rearranged to spell out the word "party" looks good.

On the inside or back of the invitation write the date, place, and starting and finishing times of the party. For small children's parties, one and a half hours is probably long enough. Three hours is a sensible limit for older children.

Costumes

Keep costumes simple and comfortable to wear. Improvise with what old clothes you may already have. Alternatively, garage sales and thrift shops are good places to find garments such as old curtains for capes and wings. Make sure they are clean!

You could start a theme party by getting the children to make something to go with their outfits, or a prop for a game. This activity can help guests get over any initial shyness and provide something for them to do while waiting for everyone to arrive.

Have everything laid out on a table ready for the children. Have all masks, buttons, and hats cut out and ready to be decorated, to avoid children using scissors. Have a good selection of shapes, sequins, feathers, glitter, glue, and felt-tip pens set out. Buttons are simple to make from circles of cardboard with a safety pin taped to the back.

Decorations

Balloons and streamers always look great at any party. Put a couple of balloons on the front door to emphasize where the party is being held. If you're holding your party outdoors, hang a bunch of balloons from a tree or bench.

For a particularly decorative look, attach a thread or string to the ceiling or walls so that it hangs above the party table, then drape streamers over it. You can adapt this idea with your theme in mind; for example, thin black plastic streamers and cut-out spiders look great at a monster party.

If you buy balloons, hang them in big bunches for a maximum effect. You could then give one to each guest as they leave.

If you want to be more ambitious and reinforce your theme, you can stick cut-out paper shapes on the windows and doors. You could hang ragged black plastic garbage bags from doorways at a monster party, tinsel for a fairy party, and green crepe paper for a jungle party.

PREPARATION 2

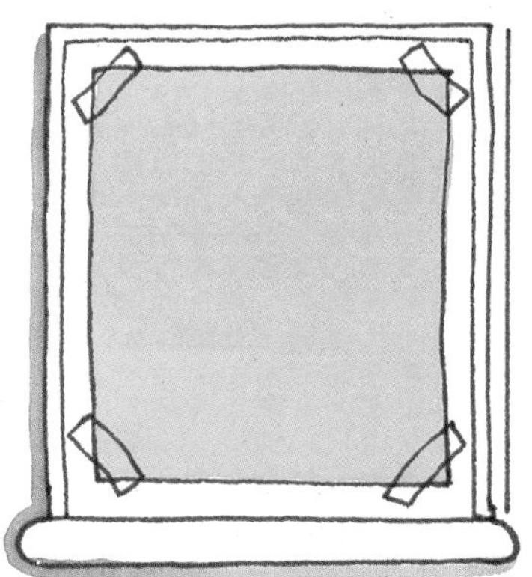

Colored crepe or tissue paper taped on windows will give off unusual light and add to the atmosphere.

You might even get your guests to help with the decorating by coloring a simple mural with felt-tip pens, outlined on drawing paper pinned to a wall. You could start the party this way. It doesn't have to be finished – your own children will enjoy finishing it if you leave it up for a few days.

Continue the theme when decorating the table. For a jungle party you can cover plates or trays with green paper leaves, or use aluminum foil for a space party. Limiting the scheme to just one or two colors is most effective.

Games

Have a list of games and a box of props and small prizes (if you want to give any) all ready before the party. Be prepared with more games than you think you will need. Try not to have gaps between the games as the children will get restless. If the weather permits, hold the party outside where there is plenty of space. You could perhaps then have a barbecue party. However, it's always a good idea to have alternative indoor games planned, in case it rains, or turns cold.

Adapt the games to fit your theme. For example, rather than play "Pin the Tail on the Donkey," you could play "Pin the Helmet on the Spaceman" at a space party, or "Pin the Star on the Fairy's Wand" at a fairy party.

Treasure hunts are always fun and can be adjusted to a theme with an appropriate prize. Children enjoy hunting for small hidden objects so these could also be chosen with the theme in mind. Hide chocolate coins at a pirate's party and small plastic animals at a jungle party.

Food

Most party food will be the same whatever party you have. But try to include a few things that are in keeping with your theme. Whatever you do, keep it simple and easy to eat, but fun and attractive.

Cookies and cupcakes are easy to make using cutters and cake tins. You can make them well in advance and keep them in the freezer.

Encourage your child to help you make the food, but discourage the use of too much dark food coloring as this will look, and be, less appetizing.

If you're having a picnic, you can pack up individual boxes (taking extra supplies for last minute "emergencies"). Buy the boxes from bakers or use old ice cream cartons.

Cake

The climax of the party is often the cake. Here you can spend a bit more time on a surprise cake to suit your theme. Using differently sized sponge cakes, jelly rolls, wafers, fondant icing, etc., all sorts of shapes and effects can be achieved.

If everyone is too full to eat a piece of cake, give out slices, wrapped in paper napkins or tinfoil, to take home.

Party Favors

Even party favors can be chosen with the theme in mind. There are endless cheap, small presents and candies to choose from. If you like you can replace the usual party bags with paper cones, small boxes, etc.

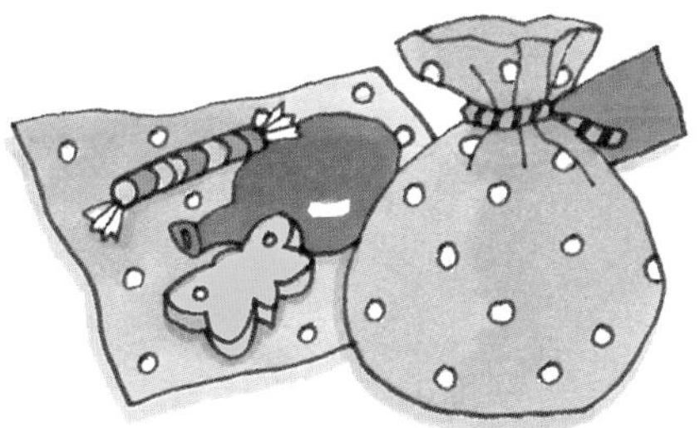

Assemble all the gifts well in advance and keep them together in a box or basket. For a personal touch you could stick on individual name labels.

CIRCUS

INVITATION

Make a Big Top Tent with opening doors, as shown.

COSTUMES

Dress up as a clown, strongman, tightrope walker, acrobat, or ringmaster.

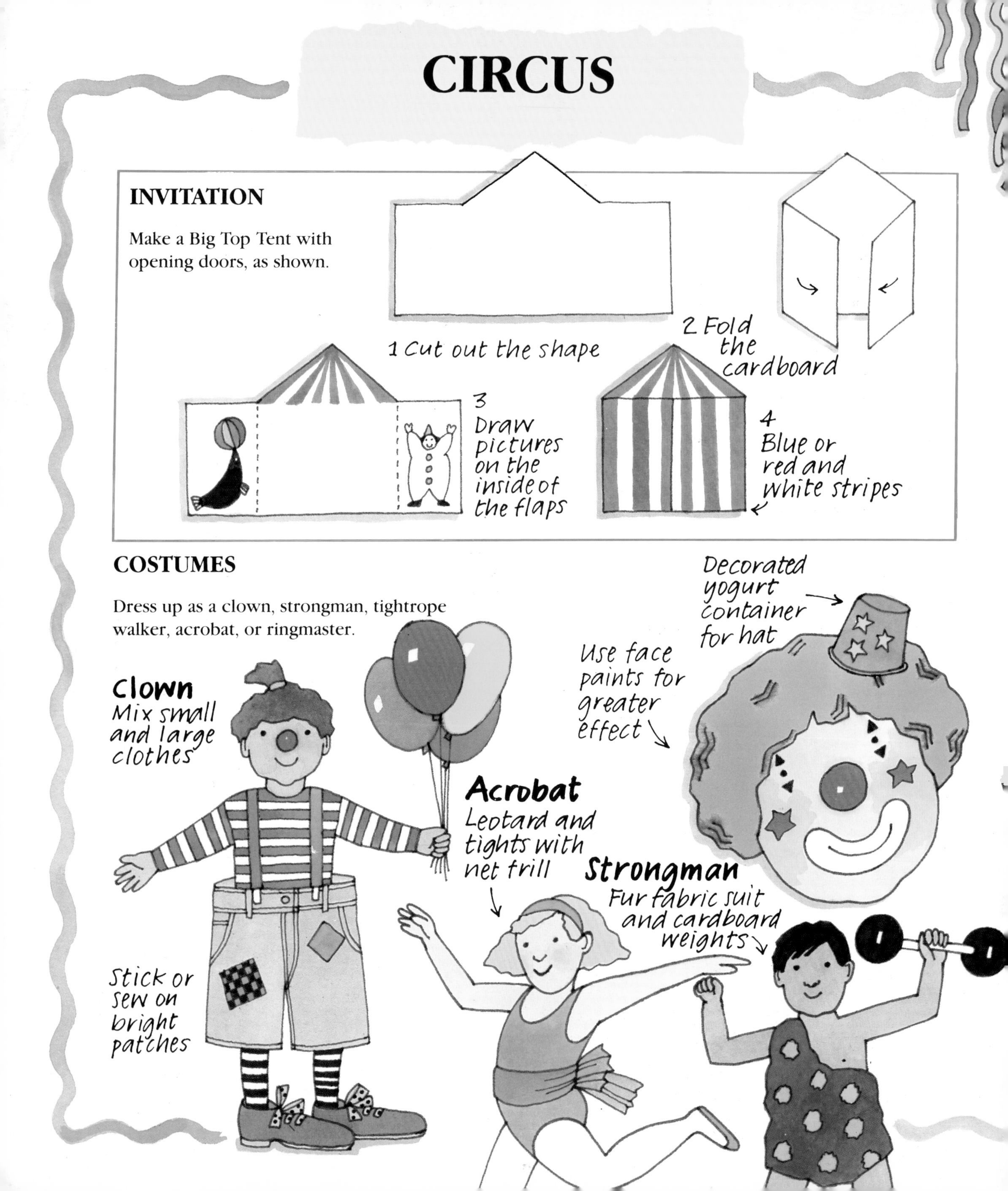

GAMES

- Make your own "Pin the Nose on the Clown's Face."
- See who can balance an object on their nose for the longest time. You could use a ball or an empty matchbox.
- Play "Ringmaster Says" as a version of "Simon Says." The "ringmaster" could wear a top hat.
- "Ring Toss." Cut rings out of cardboard and toss them over mini bags of candy laid out on the floor.

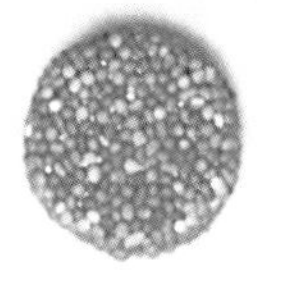

Ball of red fondant icing for nose

CAKE

Using a round sponge cake, decorate with a clown's face on top of fondant icing.

DECORATIONS

Hang up lots of brightly colored balloons and streamers.

Cut star shapes out of fondant icing

FOOD

Cut "top hat" place mats out of paper.

Serve:

- Popcorn
- Candy apples
- Cookies iced with clown faces, or cut in the shape of bow ties, spotted with candy
  - "Red noses" made from cherry tomatoes or marachino cherries stuck on cookies, or crackers with cheese or icing

PARTY FAVORS

At the end of a circus party you could give out giant balloons, noise makers, whistles, red noses, and bubbles. Buy or make simple party hats (from large yogurt containers) to put the presents in.

JUNGLE

INVITATION

Make an animal-shaped stencil. Cut out the shape or color it in.

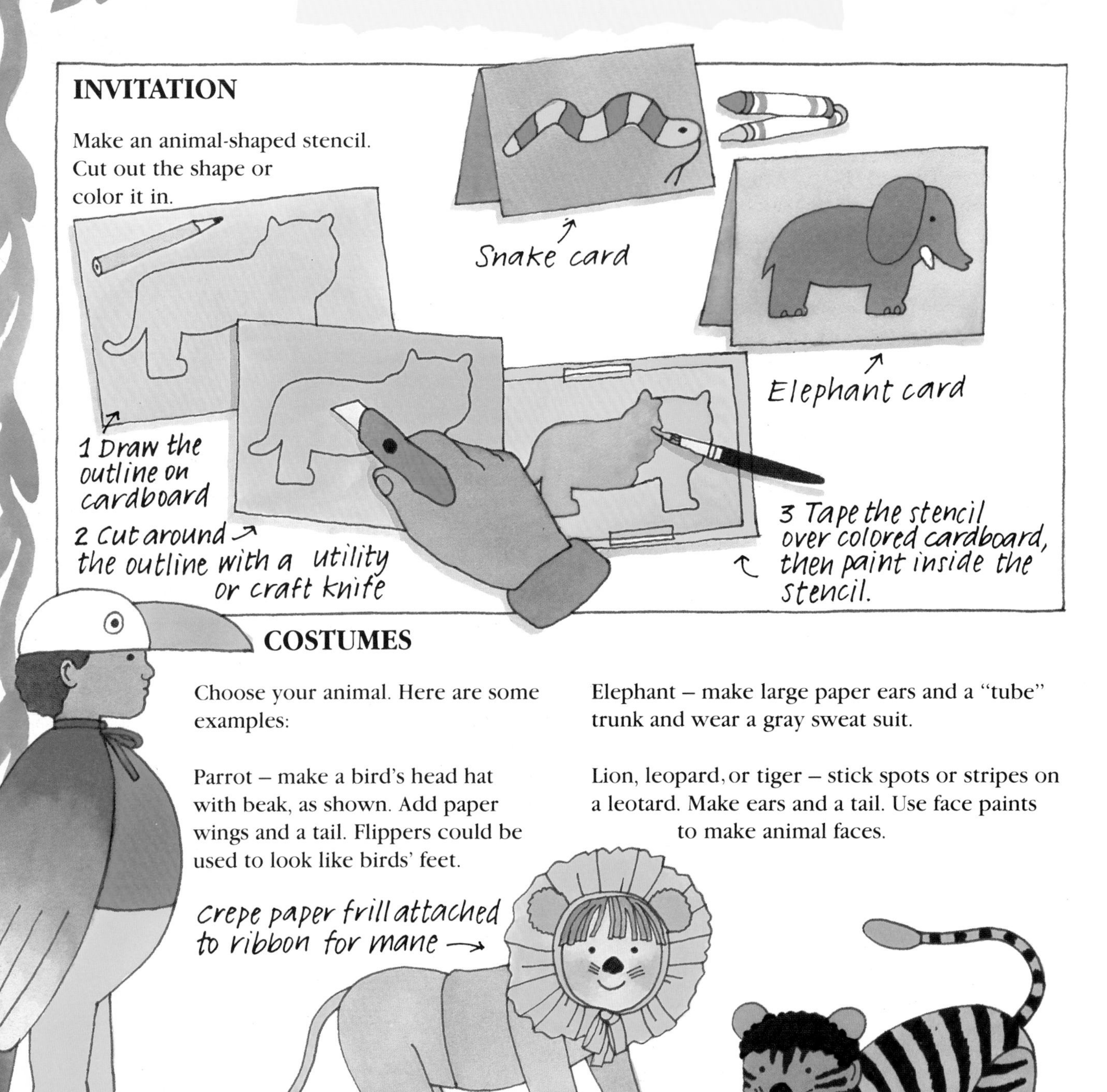

COSTUMES

Choose your animal. Here are some examples:

Parrot – make a bird's head hat with beak, as shown. Add paper wings and a tail. Flippers could be used to look like birds' feet.

Elephant – make large paper ears and a "tube" trunk and wear a gray sweat suit.

Lion, leopard, or tiger – stick spots or stripes on a leotard. Make ears and a tail. Use face paints to make animal faces.

DECORATIONS

Cut out green crepe paper leaves and brown crepe paper trunks. Then stick on huge, bright tissue or crepe paper flowers.

GAMES

- Make up an "Animal Quiz" and divide children into two teams. The team with the most correct answers is the winner. Keep questions simple.
- "What's the Time Mr Wolf?" This is a variation of "Tag" or "It." When "Mr Wolf" answers the question with, "Twelve o'clock, dinner time," the rest of the children following him must turn and run away. Whoever gets caught is the next "Mr Wolf."

PARTY FAVORS

Give out animal-shaped chocolate bars, toys, soaps, and plastic animals.

Green crepe paper bags

SUE

FOOD

Serve jungle food such as:

- Orange skin "baskets" filled with ice cream and fresh fruit
- Animal-shaped cookies
- Nuts and raisins

Wafers

CAKE

Animal faces can be made from round sponge cakes covered in butter icing. Use cookies or small cakes as ears and candy to make eyes, noses, and whiskers.

TEDDY'S PICNIC

INVITATION

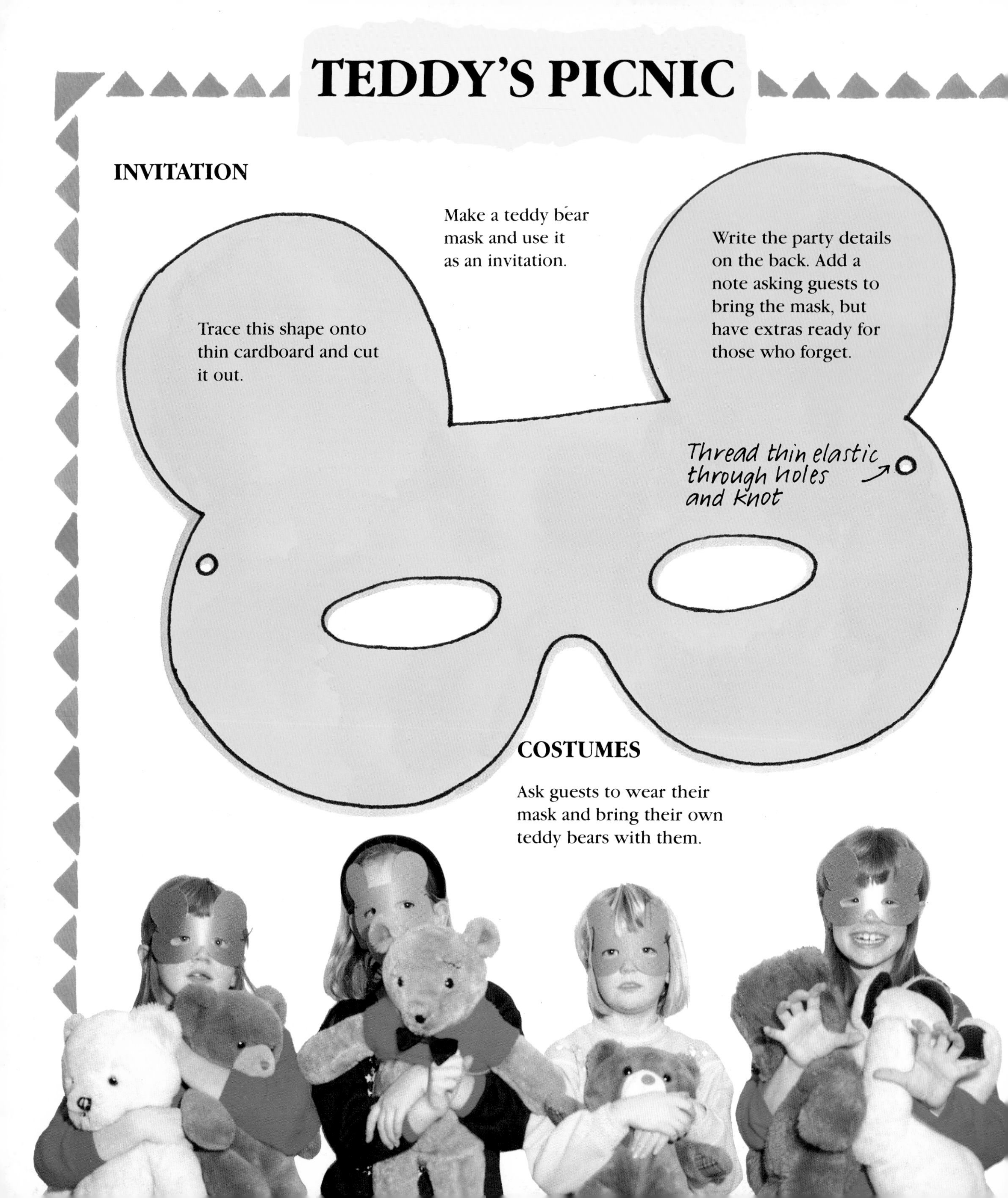

Make a teddy bear mask and use it as an invitation.

Trace this shape onto thin cardboard and cut it out.

Write the party details on the back. Add a note asking guests to bring the mask, but have extras ready for those who forget.

COSTUMES

Ask guests to wear their mask and bring their own teddy bears with them.

DECORATIONS

Tie balloons to a bench or tree by the picnic spot. Spread out a colorful tablecloth and rugs to sit on.

GAMES

- Get everyone to sing *Teddy Bear's Picnic*
- Invent games using teddy bears, for example, who can throw their bear farthest! Give winning teddy bears new ribbons.
- Act out *Goldilocks and the Three Bears*.

FOOD

Try:
- Teddy bear-shaped cookies
- Peanut butter and marmalade, or jelly sandwiches
- Honey-bran raisin muffins
- Glazed donuts

PARTY FAVORS

Buy tiny toy teddy bears, candy teddy bears, or any item with teddy bears on it. There are many picture books featuring teddy bears of various kinds, as well as Paddington, Winnie the Pooh, Rupert Bear, and other famous bear stories.

CAKE

Make a Teddy Bear cake, using one small cake for the head, a larger one for the body, cookies for ears, and "lady fingers" for the arms and legs. Cover with butter icing, positioning candy for eyes and nose.

Head
Ears
Legs
Body

MONSTER

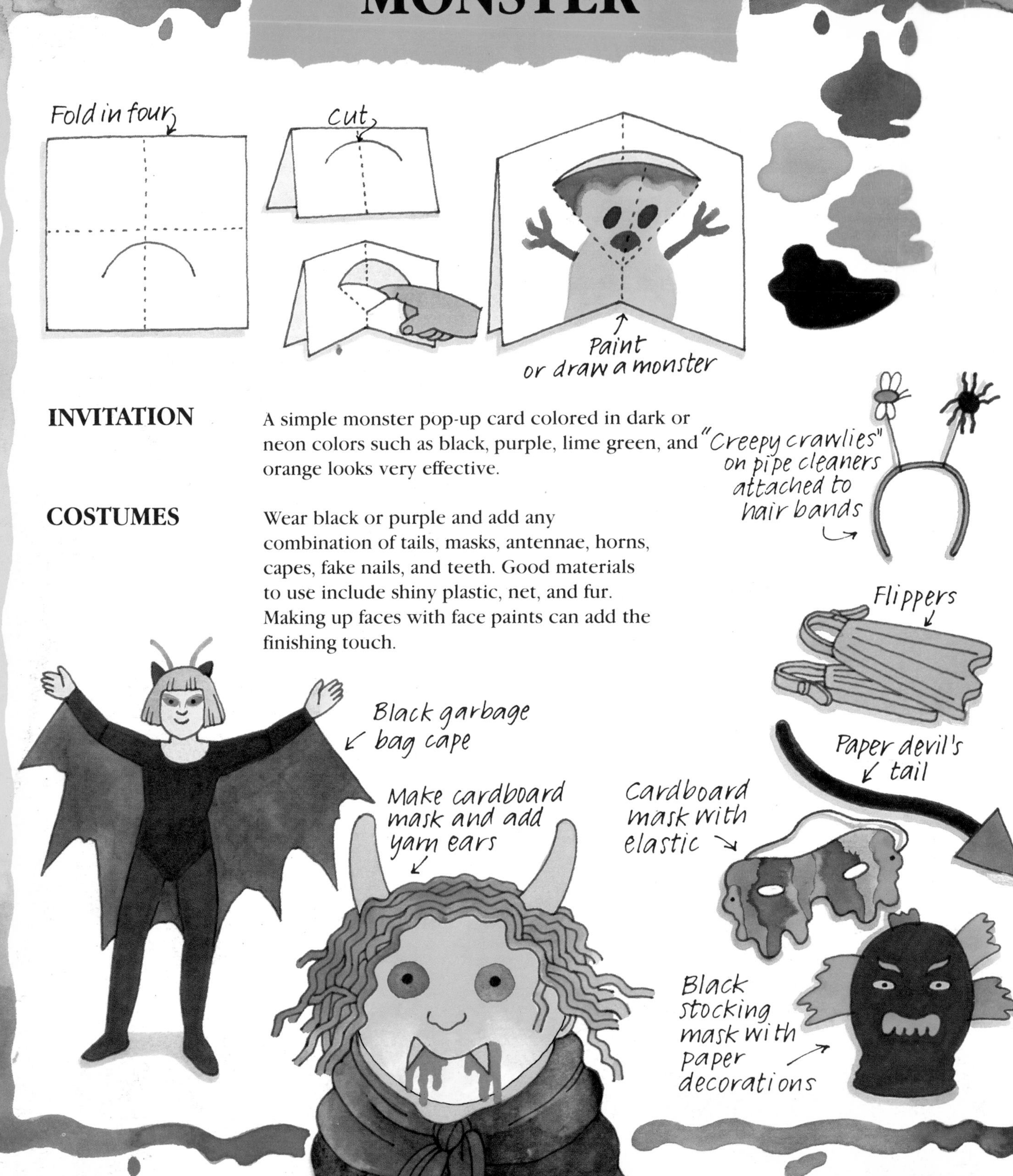

INVITATION

A simple monster pop-up card colored in dark or neon colors such as black, purple, lime green, and orange looks very effective.

COSTUMES

Wear black or purple and add any combination of tails, masks, antennae, horns, capes, fake nails, and teeth. Good materials to use include shiny plastic, net, and fur. Making up faces with face paints can add the finishing touch.

CAKE

To make a monster cake, place a small dome-shaped sponge cake on top of a round sponge cake, and then cover the shape with green runny glacé icing. Use licorice for hands and mouth, and large gumdrops for eyes.

FOOD

Serve:
• Sugar "rats" • Purple Jell-O® • Small "spider" sponge cakes or donuts with licorice "legs" • Black and green grapes

Mashed up black Jell-O®

GAMES

- Blindfold children so that they have to guess by smell and feel what certain unusually textured objects are, such as cooked spaghetti.
- Let them search with their hands for small objects hidden in mashed up Jell-O®. These games could be messy, so provide aprons and waterproof tablecloths.

DECORATIONS

Cut black garbage bags and crepe paper into tatters to hang around the room. Cover the windows in tissue paper with cut-out shapes. You could make spiders' webs out of black yarn. Hang cut-out or plastic spiders from thread strung above the table.

PARTY FAVORS

Give out "monster" candy and black balloons. Joke blood is always popular, as are plastic flies and spiders. You could also make simple monster "finger" puppets.

FAIRY

INVITATION

Cut stars out of silver and gold paper. Then stick glitter on one side and write the party details on the other.

COSTUMES

Dress in a leotard or pretty vest with a net skirt and white tights.

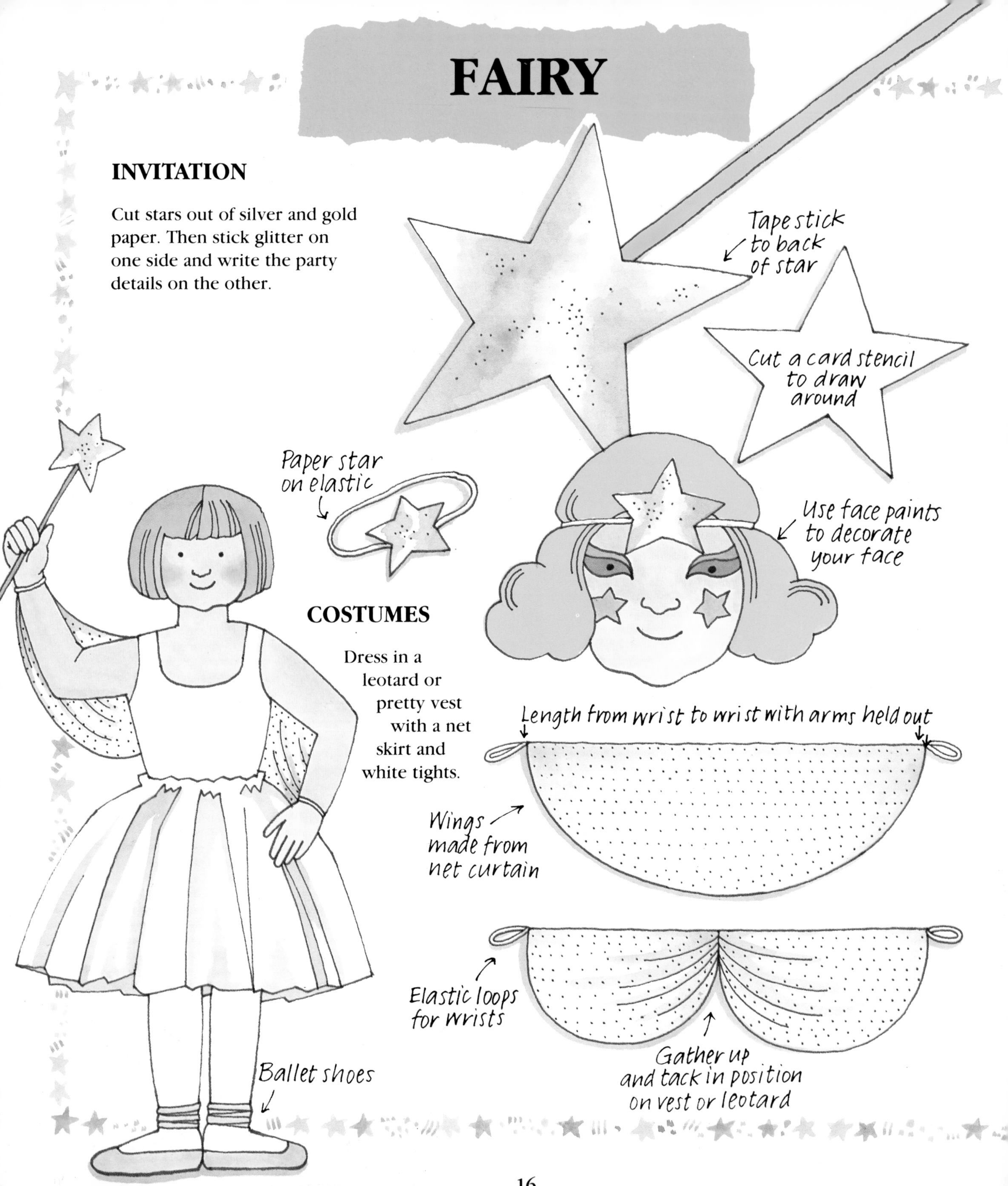

DECORATIONS

Hang tinsel above the table over a string.

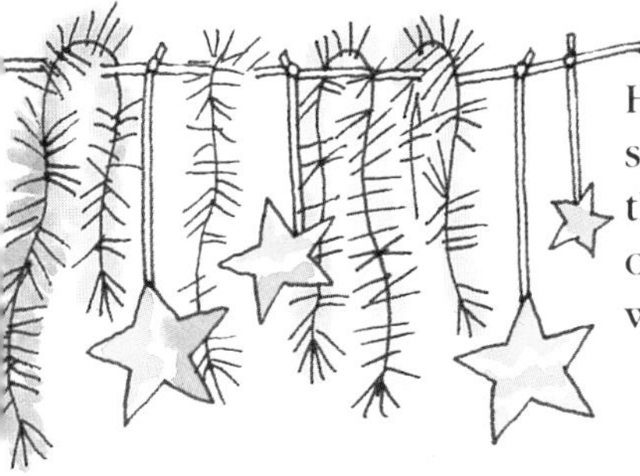

Hang silver and gold stars and moons from the ceiling on threads, or stick them to windows and doors.

GAMES

- Dancing to music.
- "Pin the Star on the Fairy's Wand."
- You could hire a magician to do a magic show or put on one of your own.

FOOD

Make or buy:
- Tiny iced cookies
- Star-shaped decorated cookies
- Cupcakes
- Pastel-colored meringue cookies stuck together with cream or jelly

CAKE

To make a fairy cake, use a dome-shaped sponge cake as a skirt. Model the fairy's body from fondant icing or insert a small plastic doll into the hollowed-out middle of cake. Cut out paper wings and make a wand from a toothpick and two stars stuck together.

PARTY FAVORS

You could make pretty cones out of paper doilies and fill them with candy wrapped in shiny metallic paper, tiny cookies, and tubes of glitter.

SPACE

INVITATION

Cut out rocket or planet shapes from cardboard.

Come to JOE'S Party

Color the shapes in and write out the party details with a silver pen. Then stick on silver and gold stars.

COSTUMES

Dress in jump suits or sweat suits, adding belts. Stick on buttons or pins and wear a helmet which you could make from a hat or a bicycle or football helmet decorated with stars and symbols.

"Laser gun" made from a plastic bottle, cardboard tube, and plastic cup.

Rubber rain or leather boots

GAMES

- Play "Pass the Space Package," wrapping the prize in layers of silver paper.
- Hold a competition to see who can draw the best "alien."

DECORATIONS

Hang up silver foil moons and stars. Buy silver balloons or spray ordinary ones with silver spray paint.

CAKE

Toy models

Paper flag on toothpick

Make a "moon cake" using a dome-shaped sponge cake covered with fondant icing. Make jagged holes in the icing for craters. For the finishing touch, stick on toy space men and space vehicles.

FOOD

- Serve individual "space meals," packed picnic-style in labeled boxes, including items such as "moon rock" cakes and sandwiches wrapped in foil

Joe

Cake box or ice cream carton

Plastic containers of fruit drinks

PARTY FAVORS

There are lots of "space theme" candies you could give out, including Mars Bars® and Milky Ways®. Or you could give toy rockets, star stickers, or books about space.

PIRATE

INVITATION

"X" marks the spot for this party! Cut out an island shape from thick paper and color one side. Then write the party details on the back. Alternatively, glue or draw a white skull and crossbones on black cardboard or construction paper.

COSTUMES

Make pirate pants from old jeans with jagged cut-off legs and patches sewn on. Add striped T-shirts and spotted bandannas. Or you could make a paper pirate's hat with skull and crossbones.

For the character Long John Silver, hop on one leg and use a wooden stick as a crutch. You could even put a toy parrot on your shoulder.

Hoop earrings sewn to scarf

Black cardboard eye patch on elastic

Rubber rain or leather boots, or bare feet depending on the weather

FOOD

You could serve:

- Boats made from roll halves covered with cream cheese or peanut butter, with paper sails on toothpicks
- Cookies iced with skull and crossbones or wrapped in colored foil to look like jewels

DECORATIONS

Cut out paper palm trees and add green paper leaves and cut-out or toy parrots.

GAMES

- Make up a "Treasure Hunt" around the house or garden to find hidden chocolate coins.
- Invent a simple secret code, using it to write clues to the whereabouts of "buried" treasure.

PARTY FAVORS

Chocolate coins, small plastic ships, eye patches, candy necklaces, bracelets, and plastic jewelry could make up pirate's treasure. As a novelty, cut up spotted cotton material into squares and tie onto a stick for them to carry it home in.

CAKE

Cut a loaf-shaped sponge cake into a prow at one end. Use brown fondant icing to cover the sides and top. Add sails and flags, using candy for portholes.

Make sails and flags out of thick paper

Wooden skewers for masts

SPOTS

INVITATION

Decorate a thick paper or cardboard circle with colored spots. You could write the party details around in a circle, too.

Lightly draw guidelines with a pair of compasses to help write your message in a circle

COSTUMES

Wear spotted clothes, or paint lots of spots on old plain clothes with fabric pens.

Stick adhesive paper circles onto fabric

Alternatives

Or you could have a striped party or a party with a theme of one particular color, and dress in appropriate clothes.

DECORATIONS

Stick or draw spots on the tablecloth, walls, paper cups, etc. Thread large paper circles on ribbons and hang them up as decorations. Or have one color for everything if you are having a one-color party.

PARTY FAVORS

Anything circular or spotted would be suitable, for example, Smarties® or any round candy, marbles, dice-shaped erasers, and sheets of sticky paper spots.

GAMES

- Hold tiddlywink races, making a circular board with a center target marked on it. The first child to flick a tiddlywink onto the target is the winner.
- Move tiddlywinks from one bowl to another by sucking them up with a straw. The child who moves the most in a given time is the winner.
- Organize a Smarties® or other kind of candy "hunt."

Plastic counters

CAKE

Use a round sponge cake, cover with butter icing, then decorate with blobs of colored glacé icing or round candy. Place small cupcakes around the main cake.

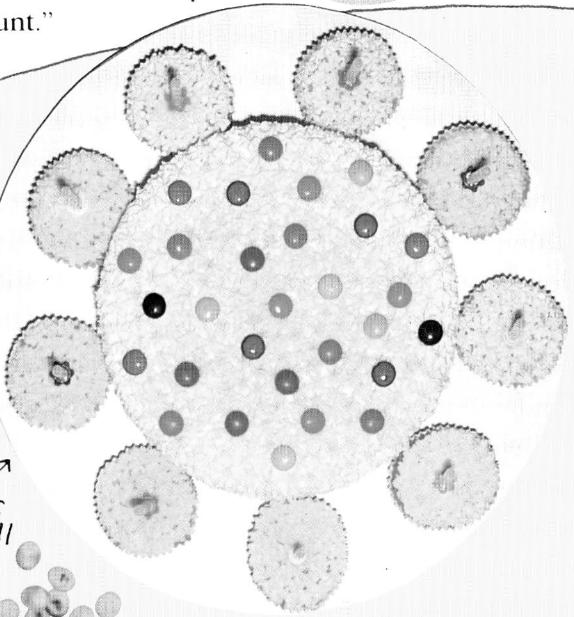

Stick candles in small cakes

FOOD

Serve:
- Round cookies decorated with round candy
- Sandwiches cut into circles with cookie cutters

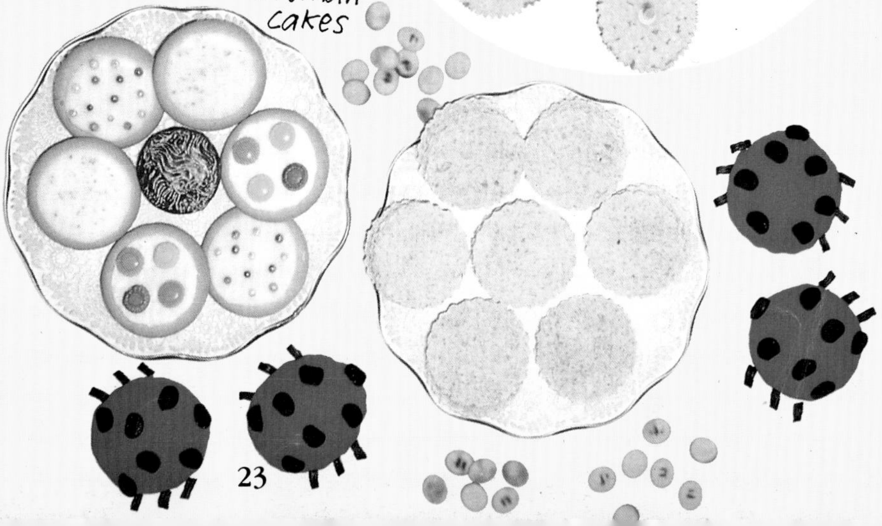

MORE IDEAS

Christmas Party

Cut out Christmas tree-shaped invitations from green paper and stick on colored spots for ornaments and glitter.

- Decorate the party room with balloons, Christmas ornaments, tinsel, and holly. Edge the food table with tinsel.
- Dress up as Santa Claus, a Christmas fairy, or as a Christmas tree dressed in green with tinsel and ornaments attached. Or go as a present dressed in red with ribbons.
- Traditional food and Christmas cookies. Or a Christmas log from a jelly roll covered in chocolate icing and dusted with confectioner's sugar "snow."
- For party favors, give out paper or material stockings filled with nuts and Christmas candies and a little wrapped present.

Swimming Party

Depending on the guests' ages, a wading pool may be sufficient. Or go to the local swimming pool. Strictly supervise the children at all times.

- Make invitations in the shape of a swimming pool, or a fish, asking guests to come in swim wear with their swimming gear.
- Play water polo with a ball, and races if you are using a swimming pool; who can throw the rubber ring the farthest, in the water or in the garden; bobbing for apples in a bowl of water.
- Picnic outside on beach towels. Make fish-shaped cookies and serve ice cream. Make a sheet cake decorated as a swimming pool or cut into a fish shape with wafer fins.

Fourth of July

- Cut out firework-shaped invitations.
- Set up a barbecue so that you can eat outdoors.
- Serve baked potatoes, hot dogs, and hamburgers, candy apples, and popcorn.
- Help children to toast marshmallows on long forks or skewers.
- Have plenty of adult helpers to organize and supervise the firework display.
- Give each child a sparkler so they can draw patterns or write their name in the air.
- The cake could be made in the shape of a rocket by standing jelly rolls on end and covering them in icing. Use wafers for wings and an ice cream cone for the nose. Or make a rectangular red, white, and blue sponge cake that resembles the flag.

Backyard "Olympic"

Divide guests into two differently colored teams, or "spotted" and "striped" teams.

- Color invitations to match – state which team the children are a member of so they come appropriately dressed.
- Hold three-legged races, wheelbarrow races and relay obstacle races.
- Give teams prizes. Have lots of games so each team wins some.
- Serve picnic cupcakes with differently colored cakes for each team.
- Give out appropriately colored "sporty" party favors, such as sunglasses, buttons, or "medals."

Party
FOOD

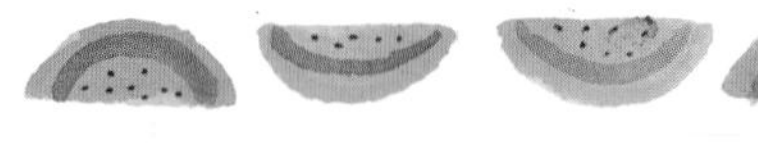

2 · FOOD

INTRODUCTION

The best party food is fun and easy to eat. Keep ideas simple and colorful. If you are having a party with a theme, you could make some of the food to match.

Sandwiches, cookies, gelatin, and ice cream are always popular at any children's party. With the main components of a party in mind, this section has been divided into separate topics to give you lots of novel but simple ideas to choose from.

Much of the food can be cooked or prepared in advance, and kept in the freezer or airtight containers. Cakes and cookies can be iced and decorated the morning before the party.

Many children get too excited at parties to eat large amounts, so don't overdo the quantities. Bite-size "nibbles" usually go down well with children as they can try a bit of everything.

It's a good idea to have a variety of "real" foods as well as "treats" on the table to cater to different tastes. Food cut or arranged in novel shapes will appeal most to children.

It's also a good idea to set individual places at the table for each guest. Provide plenty of colorful napkins, as most of the party food will be eaten with their fingers.

Color is perhaps the most important thing to consider when preparing a children's party. Bright colors always look good, but avoid using too many dark colors as these will look less appetizing.

Natural food colorings are available so read labels carefully and avoid those with high sugar, preservative, or artificial ingredient contents.

Other ingredients to avoid include whole nuts and anything that could get stuck in children's throats. Also beware of serving strong tasting or spicy food to children. It's safer to make simple dishes and concentrate on decorating and presenting them attractively.

TABLE DECOR

The food table is usually the central attraction of the party, so decorate it with special care. If you are having a party with a theme, it adds to the fun to try and match the table decor and some of the food to it. For example, at a space party you could cover the table and plates with silver foil and dangle cardboard planets and moons from a string strung above the table. However you decide to decorate your table, make sure it is well covered with waterproof tablecloths and always provide plenty of paper napkins.

Place mats

Novelty-shaped individual place mats can be cut out of cardboard or thick paper. Simply use a stencil or tracing, or draw around an appropriate object. Make large circles for a spotted party, or top hats for a circus party, and get the children to color and decorate their own when they arrive.

Place cards

To avoid any arguments over where everyone is to sit, it is a good idea to put a place card with each guest's name on it on the table before they arrive. The birthday child may enjoy writing these on folded pieces of cardboard and perhaps drawing the person's face, too. Again, if you are having a theme, you could cut the cards into the appropriate shapes.

Plates and cups

You can buy many different kinds of patterned plastic and paper party cups and plates. However, you may prefer to decorate some with stickers yourself. Do not use spray paints or pens to color anything that will come in contact with food, as they may be toxic.

Hats and masks

You could make or buy a party hat or mask for each child and have them ready to wear beside their place at the table. These could match your theme if you're having one. Children also love having noise makers and streamers to play with at the table.

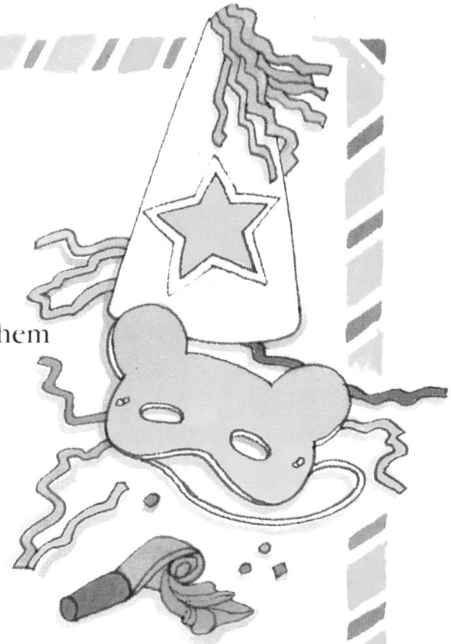

Finishing touches

Put flexible straws and paper umbrellas in drinks for a fun touch. Place bite-sized pieces of food on toothpicks and stick into halved grapefruits or oranges for a "porcupine" effect. When you are ready for the cake, dim the lights, and make a grand entrance with candles alight.

SANDWICHES

Children find sandwiches made from thinly sliced bread easier to eat. Make a variety of different fillings, clearly marked.

Make the sandwiches on the day of the party, keeping them well covered so they don't dry out. Garnish them at the last minute with condiments, lettuce and tomato.

There are plenty of novel ways you can serve sandwiches to make them more appealing. Try cutting them into different shapes using cookie cutters.

SANDWICH WHEELS

Cut the crusts off slices of pumpernickel or white bread. Then, with a rolling pin, roll the slices out lightly and spread thickly with cream cheese. Place a stick of celery across one end of each slice and roll up tightly. Wrap the rolls in foil until just before eating. Then cut them into ½ in, (10 mm) slices to serve.

CHEESEBOARD

Arrange small squares of pumpernickel and white sandwiches like a chessboard.

CROISSANTS

Croissants can be filled with fruit, meat, or cheese. You could also use bagels and differently flavored breads. Let the guests "decorate" their own bread or bagels with fruits, vegetables, peanut butter, or cream cheese.

OPEN SANDWICHES

Open sandwiches can be endlessly varied and look very colorful and attractive. Don't overload the bread or the topping will fall off.

ROLL BOATS

Slice rolls in half, butter, and spread with filling. Then add toothpick "masts" and paper "sails."

LABELS

Cut out appropriate shapes from paper as labels to stick into plates of sandwiches using toothpicks.

SANDWICH HOUSE

A sandwich house is simple to construct and makes a fun centerpiece on the table. Cut square sandwiches for the main building, arranging them in a solid block as big as you like, but not higher than three sandwiches, or they will fall over. Cut triangular sandwiches for the roof, buttering both sides of the bread to help stick the sandwiches together (toothpicks can also be used to help secure the sandwiches). Cut vegetables for windows, doors, etc.

CUPCAKES

Bake lots of small cupcakes. You can freeze them if you want to make them in advance.

SPONGE MIXTURE

To make about 16 cupcakes you will need . . .

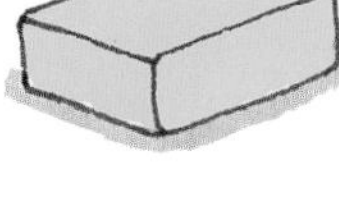

- 6 oz. (175 g) softened butter or margarine
- 6 oz. (175 g) super fine sugar

- 3 eggs
- 6 oz. (175 g) self-rising flour

Set the oven at 350°F (180°C). Put the softened butter and sugar in a mixing bowl and beat with a wooden spoon until the mixture is pale and creamy. Beat the eggs separately, then add them to the butter and sugar mixture a little at a time, stirring well until smooth. Sift the flour into the mixture and mix well.

Spoon the mixture into individual paper cupcake or muffin cups and smooth level. Bake in the oven for 15-20 minutes until risen and golden brown.

CHOCOLATE CRISPIES

"Chocolate crispies" are popular with children, both to make and eat. They are very easy to make as no baking is required.

Simply melt some chocolate in a bowl, then stir in cornflakes or rice crispies. Place large spoonfuls in cupcake or muffin cups and allow to cool and harden.

GLACÉ ICING

Glacé icing is easy to make and can be used to decorate cakes and cookies. Sift confectioner's sugar into a bowl. Add hot water a little at a time, mixing it with the sugar to make a smooth paste.

Use a wet knife to help spread it. You can add food coloring to glacé icing, or make a chocolate variation by replacing a quarter of the confectioner's sugar with cocoa.

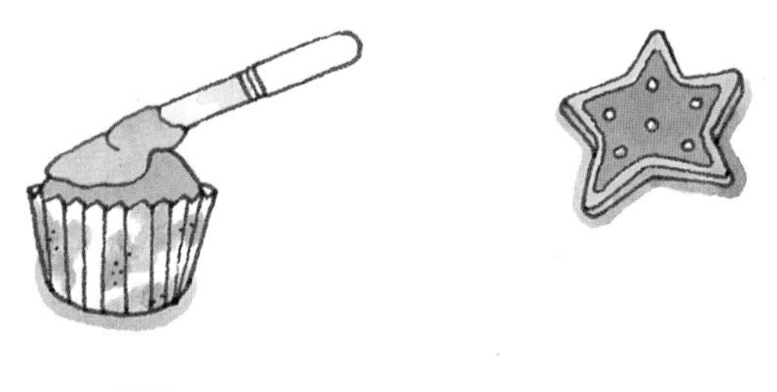

Color glacé icing with food colorings

BUTTERFLY CAKES

Make the cupcakes as usual. Then, when cool, carefully cut a shallow hole out of the top of each. Fill the hole with butter icing. To make the butterfly wings slice the cut-off top piece in two and stick the straight edges together into the icing at an angle.

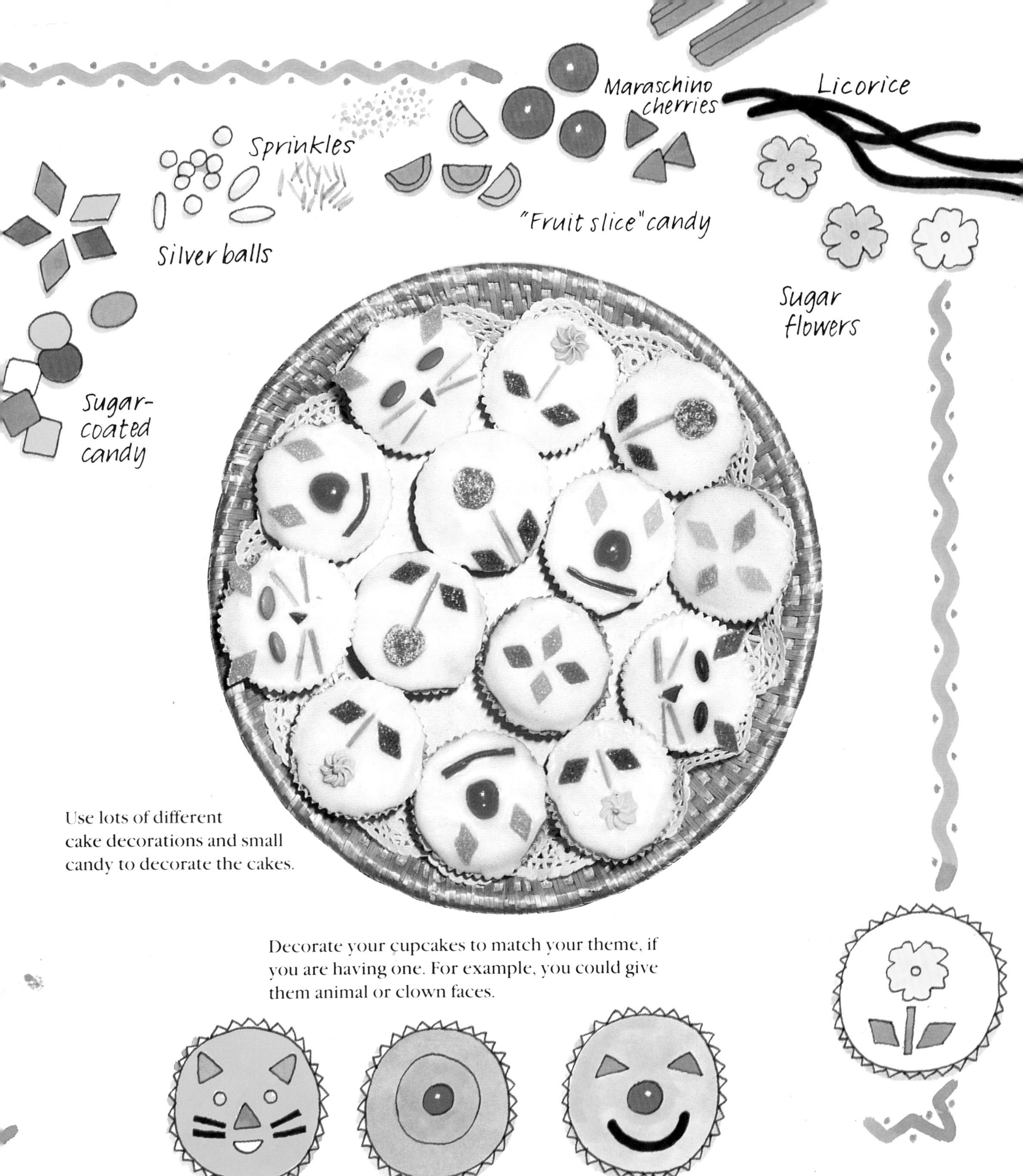

Use lots of different cake decorations and small candy to decorate the cakes.

Decorate your cupcakes to match your theme, if you are having one. For example, you could give them animal or clown faces.

GELATINS

Individual Jell-O® gelatins in paper dishes are pretty. Make several different flavors. You can add a little chopped up fruit at the bottom and a blob of whipped cream on top.

A large molded gelatin makes an amusing centerpiece, though looks rather messy once cut.

Pink rabbit with "mashed" green Jell-O® around it on a plate

MILK JELL-O®

Melt gelatin in hot water as normal, then top up to required amount with fresh or evaporated milk. For a striped effect, make half with water, leave it to set, then add a layer of gelatin milk mixture.

MAGIC JELL-O®

You will need...

Large oranges
Packets of differently flavored gelatins

Cut the oranges in two and carefully scoop all the flesh out of the halves. Stand the empty skins on trays.

Use bits of adhesive putty to hold up the fruit.

Use differently colored gelatins

Then make the Jell-O®. Don't use quite so much water as instructed on the packet to ensure it sets firmly. Pour into the orange skins up to the top. When set, carefully cut each orange half into three segments.

The segments "magically" have Jell-O® inside the real orange skin. It's fun to make lots of different colors.

Look for gelatin moulds in different fun shapes and sizes.

Make Jell-O® "boats" using toothpicks and paper "sails."

STRIPED JELL-O®

Set different colored layers of gelatin in glasses for a striped effect. Allow each new layer to set before adding the next color.

JELL-O® KEBABS

Set differently colored gelatins in metal ice cube trays with the divider removed (or in a shallow plastic tray). Use slightly less liquid than instructed on the packet. Then cut into cubes and thread onto skewers.

DRINKS

If you want to be more adventurous with drinks than basic juices and soda, here are some simple recipes to try:

MILKSHAKES

You will need...

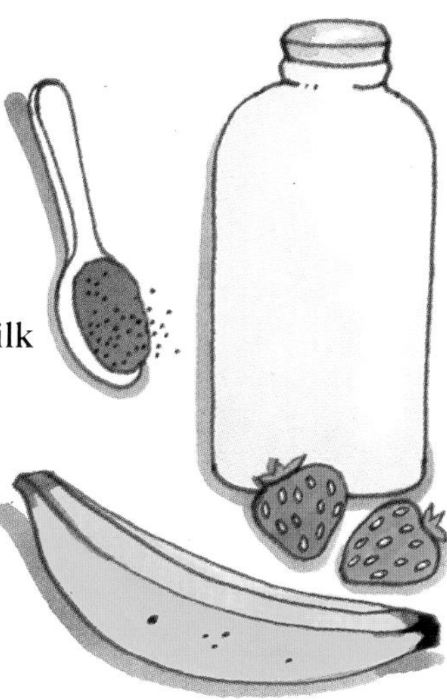

12 oz. (350 g) fresh fruit
2 tablespoons super fine sugar
1½ pints (900 ml) milk
4 scoops vanilla ice cream

Place half the fruit, sugar, milk, and ice cream in a blender or food processor. Blend for 20 seconds, then pour into a pitcher. Repeat with the remaining ingredients. This recipe makes 2 pints (1.2 liters) of natural, creamy milkshake. Serve in tall glasses with straws.

ICE CREAM SODAS

Fill glasses half full with lemonade, then add scoops of ice cream. You could also use orange juice or soda.

FRUIT PUNCH

Top glasses of fruit juice with lemonade. In the winter you could make a hot punch with apple cider, orange juice, cinnamon, and water.

HOT CHOCOLATE

Marshmallows floating in hot chocolate make a delicious treat in the winter. Alternatively, spray whipped cream on top of a hot chocolate drink and grate chocolate on top, or dot with colored sprinkles. Serve with teaspoons.

Whipped cream
Marshmallows

HOMEMADE LEMONADE

For a refreshing and natural lemonade try this quick and easy recipe:

You will need...

4 lemons
3 oz. (75 g) super fine sugar
2 pints (1.2 liters) boiling water

Grate the rind from the lemons and place in a heatproof pitcher with the sugar. Pour the water and stir until the sugar has dissolved. Squeeze the lemons and strain into the container. Allow to cool. Makes 2 pints (1.2 liters).

MAGIC POTION

For a very fizzy effect, freeze chocolate chips and place a few at the bottom of each glass. Then fill the glasses with soda.

Put slices of orange and lemon on the rim of glasses
Dip the rims of glasses in lemon juice, then sugar or coconut
Make decorations for straws. Keep them simple and place near the top of the straw.
Tissue flowers
Butterfly
Names
Cleo
Tinsel
Paper fruit
Spider
Bat

PIZZAS

You can make pizza crusts well in advance and freeze them. When ready to cook, cover the dough in a tomato sauce (see recipe below). All the additional toppings can be selected and added by the children at the party. Let them do this between games so the pizzas can be ready to eat from the oven when the meal starts.

PIZZA DOUGH

This recipe makes two 4 in. (10 cm) pizza crusts

You will need...

6 oz. (175 g) self-rising flour
Pinch of salt and pepper
1½ oz. (40 g) butter or margarine
2 oz. (50 g) grated cheese
3-4 tablespoons milk

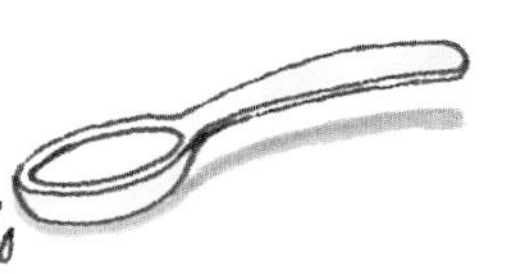

Chop up the butter and place in a bowl with the flour and seasoning. Rub in the butter until the mixture looks like breadcrumbs. Add the grated cheese and the milk and mix it all together until you have a small ball of dough. Divide the dough in half and roll out into 4 in. (10 cm) circles. Once the pizza dough has been covered with tomato sauce and toppings, bake for 15 minutes at 425°F (220°C) until the edges are golden brown.

Have the dough already placed on baking trays if the children are going to decorate their own. To prevent confusion you could get the children to make distinguishing marks in their decoration, or mark their initials in tinfoil tucked under their own pizza pies.

PIZZA SAUCE

You will need...

1 small onion
1 small can of tomatoes
1 tablespoon of tomato pureé
Pinch of salt and pepper

Mash up the whole tomatoes with a fork and mix in the tomato pureé, (or put into a blender or food processor for a few seconds). Heat the mixture together with the chopped onion and seasoning for 15 minutes in a saucepan. Allow the sauce to cool before spreading on the pizza dough.

MINI PIZZAS

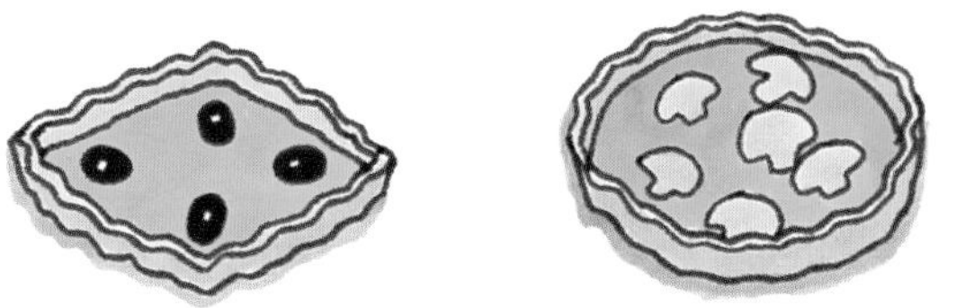

Bagels, English muffins, or Italian bread slices can be used to make mini pizzas. Add tomato sauce and toppings in the normal way.

Names on tinfoil

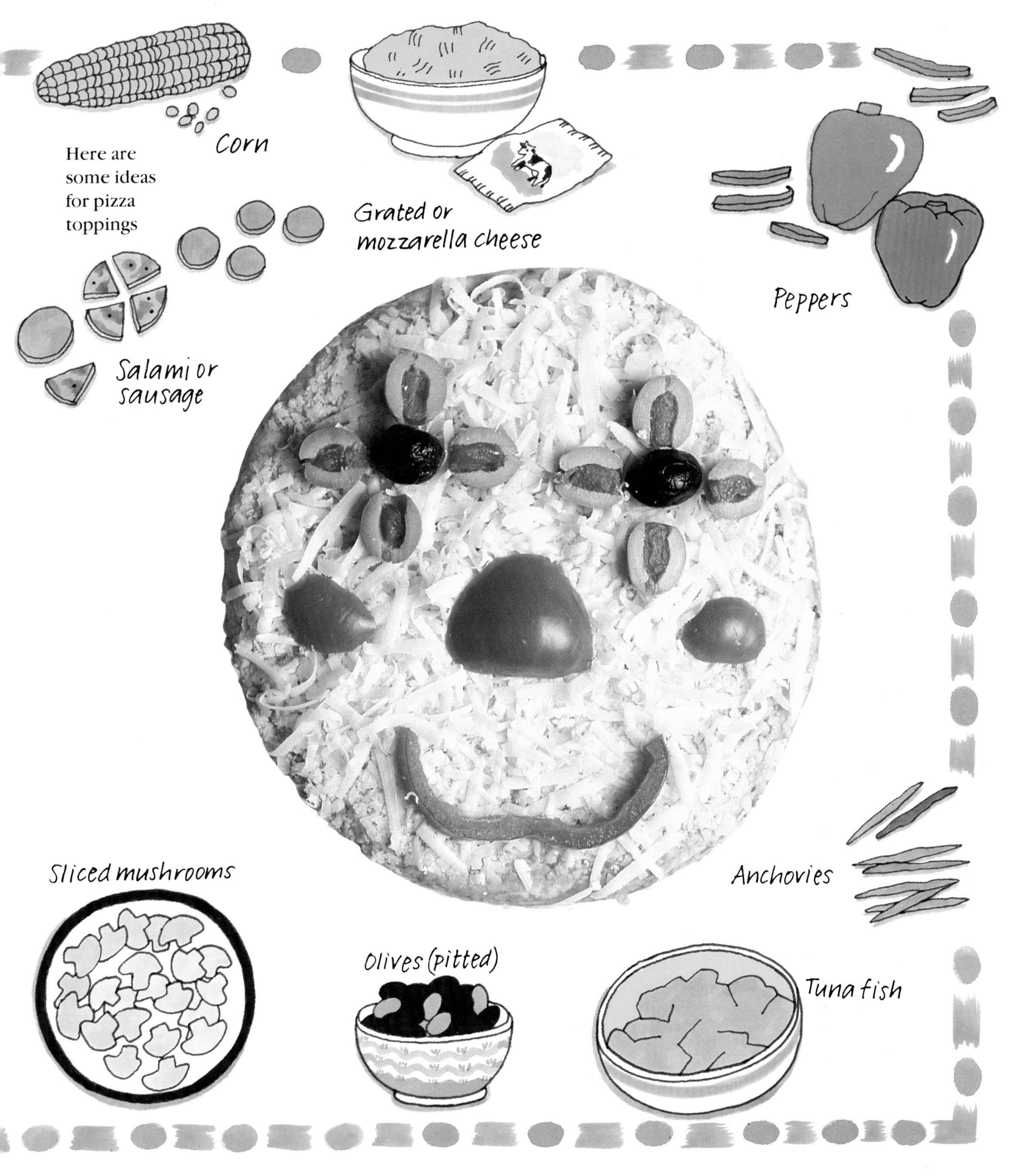
Corn
Here are
some ideas
for pizza
toppings
Grated or
mozzarella cheese
Peppers
Salami or
sausage
Sliced mushrooms
Anchovies
Olives (pitted)
Tuna fish

FRUIT

Most children love fresh fruit. What you choose to serve obviously depends on the season. Canned, dried, or frozen fruit can also be used. Many fruits are now canned in their natural juice rather than syrup, which is healthier.

FRUIT KEBABS

Dip small fruits, such as strawberries, grapes, or tangerine segments, half way into melted chocolate. Leave them until the chocolate has hardened, then thread onto toothpicks to serve.

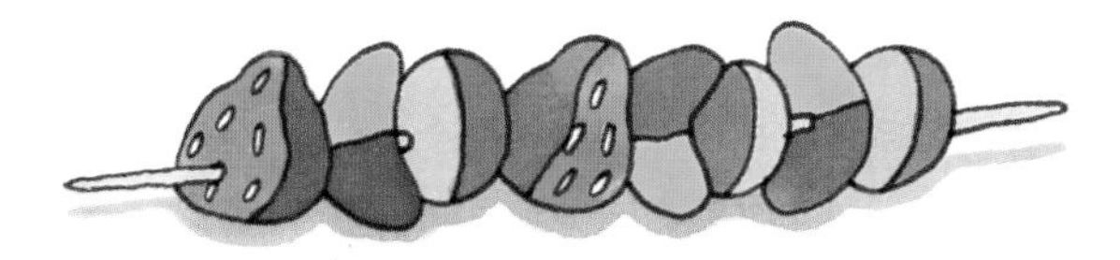

BANANAS

Bananas are especially popular with children. For a special treat, dip whole bananas in melted chocolate and then roll them in colored sprinkles.

You can also bake bananas in their skins, either in the oven or in the embers of a barbecue, until the skins are blackened. Peel back a strip of skin when cool enough to eat and serve on a plate with whipped cream and brown sugar.

Make sure the bananas are cool enough to serve

CANDY APPLES

You will need...

14 short wooden (ice cream) sticks
14 medium dessert apples
1lb. (450g) dark brown sugar
3 oz. (75 g) butter or margarine
2 teaspoons white or cider vinegar
6 fl. oz. (175 ml) water
2 tablespoons light corn syrup

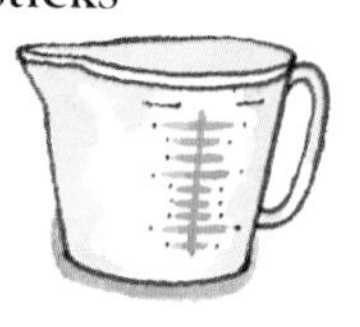

Push a stick firmly onto the core of each apple. Heat the other ingredients gently in a large saucepan until the sugar has dissolved. Bring to the boil for 5 minutes, without stirring, until a little mixture dropped into cold water becomes hard. Remove from the heat and stand in cold water to stop the mixture from cooking.

Dip the apples one at a time into the mixture. Lift each apple out and twirl over the pan until evenly coated with toffee. Place on an oiled baking sheet until "candy" mixture has hardened.

FRUIT SALAD

Cut the top off a pineapple and carefully scoop out the flesh. Cut the flesh into cubes and mix it with other fruit. Fill the pineapple with the fruit. Keep in the refrigerator until ready to serve.

You could use a melon instead of a pineapple

Pour a little orange juice over the fruit salad

Lemon juice stops fruit from browning

Cut large fruit into cubes or use whole small fruits. Put onto toothpicks and push into half a grapefruit or a large orange.

BARBECUE

Barbecues are fun either for a summer lunch or a Fourth of July celebration, or in the winter as part of a Christmas party. If you don't want to cook a lot, even hot dogs and warmed pita bread will make a nice change and are easy. Afterward the children can toast marshmallows. Remember to always have an adult in charge of the barbecue to avoid any accidents.

KEBABS

Cut chicken, pork, or beef into cubes and thread alternately onto metal skewers. For extra flavor, marinate the meat for several hours before cooking (see recipe).

Add vegetables such as cherry tomatoes, onions, and chunks of pepper for a bit of color.

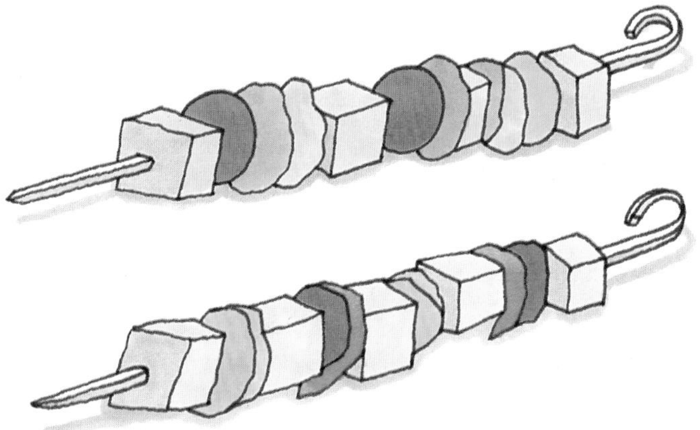

MARINADE

HONEY AND ORANGE

You will need...

2 tablespoons honey
1 tablespoon Worcestershire sauce
Grated rind and juice of ½ orange
1 tablespoon tomato pureé
1 tablespoon soy sauce

Mix all the ingredients together in a bowl and brush over chicken, beef or pork. Cover the meat completely in tinfoil and marinate for at least 1 hour before cooking. Use any remaining sauce to baste the meat while it is on the grill.

POTATO SKINS

Cut baked potatoes in half and scoop out the insides. Mash them together with grated cheese and butter or margarine and spoon back into the skins. Garnish with sour cream and chives, or use toothpicks and slices of cheese and pepper to make "boats."

PITAS

Mini "party" pitas are a good alternative to burger buns as small children will find them fun and easier to eat. Warm them up in the oven first, then slit open one end and fill with salad, pieces of hamburgers or vegiburgers, and slices of cheese. Serve with a paper napkin.

A BARBECUE CAFÉ

Write a menu on a blackboard or piece of cardboard and serve your guests from a table.

"PIG IN A BLANKET"

A "pig in a blanket" is an original way to barbecue sausages or hot dogs. Wrap a couple of slices of bacon around each hot dog, leaving the ends sticking out. Use toothpicks to secure the ends. Cook over the barbecue.

Chestnuts are good to roast at the end of a winter barbecue. Eat them with salt and butter.

COOKIES

Cookies are very popular and easy to make. A tray of these in different shapes, iced, and brightly decorated, is ideal for children to take to school on their birthday.

BUTTER COOKIES

To make 20 cookies
you will need...

4 oz. (100 g) butter or
margarine
4 oz. (100 g) super
fine sugar
1 egg
8 oz. (225 g) plain flour
Rind from 1 lemon,
finely grated

Set the oven at 350°F (180°C). Cream the butter and sugar together until light and fluffy. Then beat in the egg gradually. Stir in the sieved flour and lemon rind to form a stiff dough. Knead the dough lightly and roll out to ¼ in. (5 mm) thick. Cut into shapes and place on lightly greased baking trays. Bake until a light golden color. When cooked, place them on a wire rack to cool.

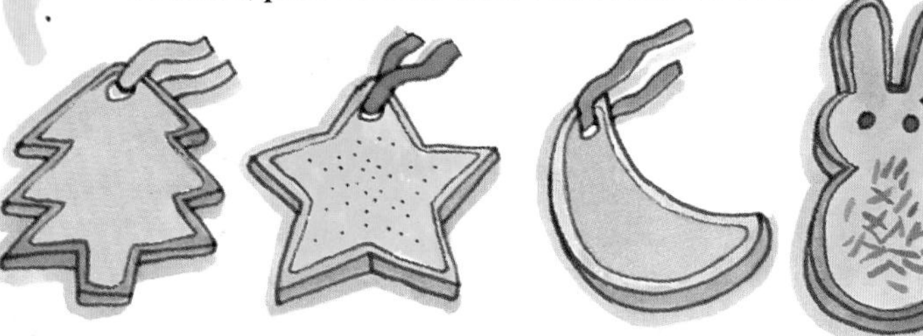

Make a hole with a skewer in the top of the cookies before cooking. When cooked and allowed to cool, thread with ribbon or yarn and hang up or give out as party favors.

SPICY COOKIES

To make 24 cookies
you will need...

10 oz. (275 g) self-
rising flour
1 tablespoon of
cinnamon
4 oz. (100 g) light brown
sugar
3 oz. (75 g) butter or
margarine
1 small egg
2 oz. (50 g) light
corn syrup

Set the oven at 325°F (170°C). Sift the flour and cinnamon into a mixing bowl, then stir in the sugar. Cut up the butter and rub it into the mixture until it looks like breadcrumbs. Beat the egg separately with a fork and then add the corn syrup to it, mixing until smooth. Make a hole in the flour mixture and pour in the egg mixture. Mix together until you have a big ball of dough. Place the dough in a plastic bag and keep in the refrigerator for 30 minutes. Roll out, cut, and bake as with butter cookies.

Children will love to help cut out the cookies in different shapes and decorate them by pressing chopped nuts, raisins, or sesame seeds into the dough. When cooked you can decorate with icing, cake decorations, and candy.

Using the spicy cookie recipe, make gingerbread people and write the guests' names on them, using tubes of icing.

You could dip some cookies half into melted chocolate

Decorate the cookies with candy and raisins

Arrange lots of different cookies on a plate

Make cookies to match the theme of your party.

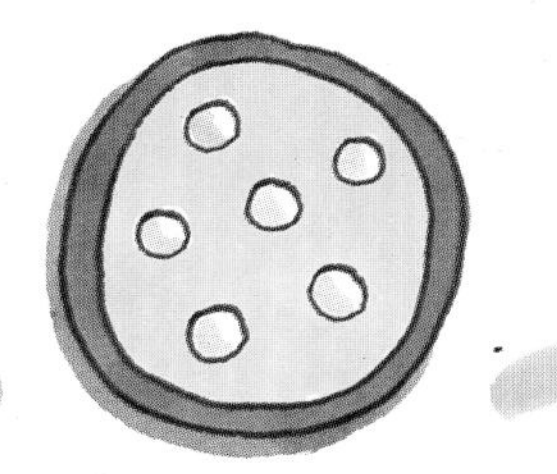

ICE CREAM

Most children enjoy ice cream or its less-fattening "relative," frozen yogurt. Whether you make your own or buy it, serving ice cream and frozen yogurt with a sauce makes it extra special for a party. These sauce recipes can be made a few days in advance and kept in the refrigerator.

BUTTERSCOTCH SAUCE

You will need...

10 fl. oz. (285 ml) heavy cream
4 oz. (100 g) unsalted butter
6 oz. (175 g) light brown sugar

Place all the ingredients in a saucepan. Heat gently, stirring until the sugar has dissolved. Then bring to a boil and boil for 2 minutes, until syrupy. Serve hot or cold.

MAKING SUNDAES

Put various flavors of ice cream or frozen yogurt, the sauces, and as many toppings as you like out on a table so the children can construct their own sundaes. Try to avoid a shoving match and have the table and surrounding area well covered! Alternatively, put single scoops of ice cream or yogurt in small bowls and decorate as faces or animals.

CHOCOLATE SAUCE

You will need...

6 oz. (175 g) plain chocolate, chopped
2 oz. (50 g) super fine sugar
8 fl. oz. (250 ml) milk

Place all the ingredients in a saucepan and heat gently, stirring until the sugar has dissolved. Simmer for 2 to 3 minutes. Serve hot or cold.

RASPBERRY SAUCE

You will need...

6 oz. (175 g) raspberries, fresh or frozen
3 oz. (75 g) super fine sugar

Wash the raspberries and push them through a sieve over a bowl using a wooden spoon. Add the sugar to the raspberry pulp a little at a time. Then stir the sauce vigorously until all the sugar has dissolved. Serve hot or cold.

MARS BAR® SAUCE

For a very quick and delicious sauce, gently melt Mars Bars® in a saucepan with a little milk.

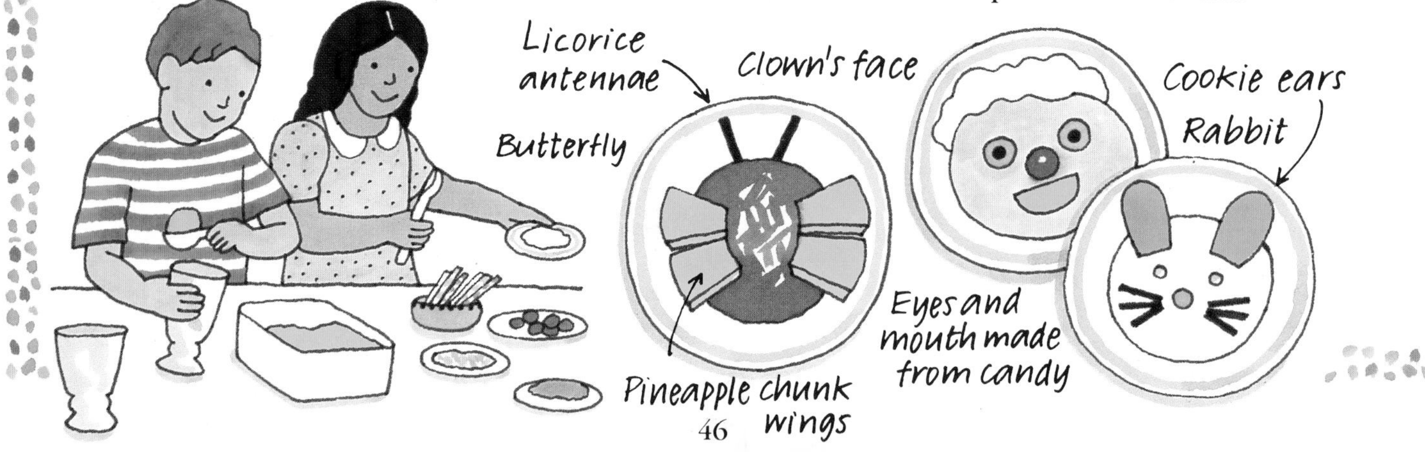

Add a miniature umbrella for a final, fun touch

Put all the toppings into small bowls or saucers with a spoon in each.

Chopped fruit, fresh or canned

Sprinkles

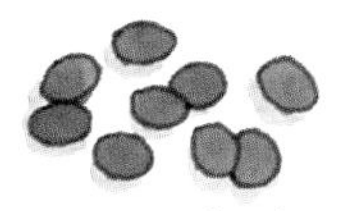

Chocolate chips

Chopped nuts

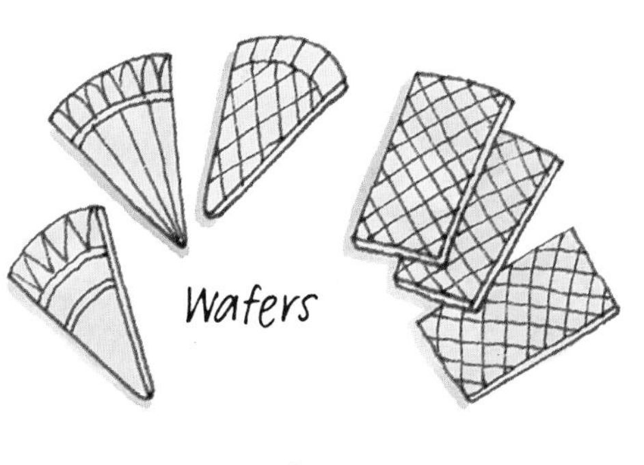

Wafers

"Lady fingers"

Chocolate logs

Maraschino cherries

Whipped cream is the easiest to use

Use thick glasses or glass dessert dishes if you can't get sundae glasses

SALADS

Children can be very fussy about eating salad and fresh vegetables, so take extra care to present vegetables in a novel and attractive way. Make use of the naturally colorful varieties for decoration.

VEGETABLE SHAPES

Cut brightly colored vegetables, such as peppers, carrots, and tomatoes, into shapes and use to garnish plates of sandwiches. You could also thread chunks onto toothpicks to make vegetable kebabs.

VEGETABLE KEBABS

Vegetable shapes and small vegetables such as radishes look good threaded alternately onto skewers.

TOMATOES

Scoop the insides out of cherry tomatoes and fill them with cream cheese. You can have fun arranging the tomatoes in amusing and interesting patterns, for example, the age of the birthday child.

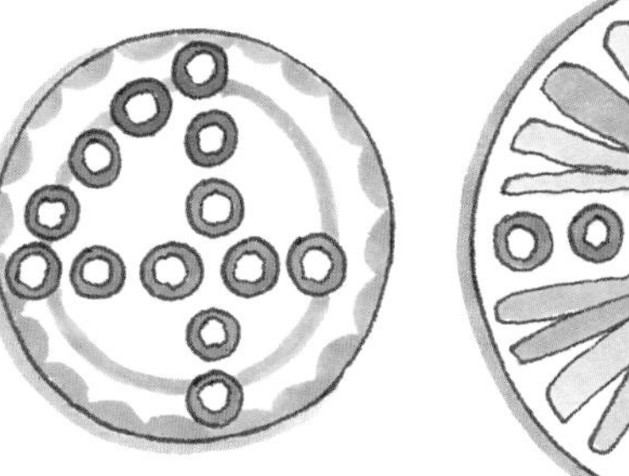

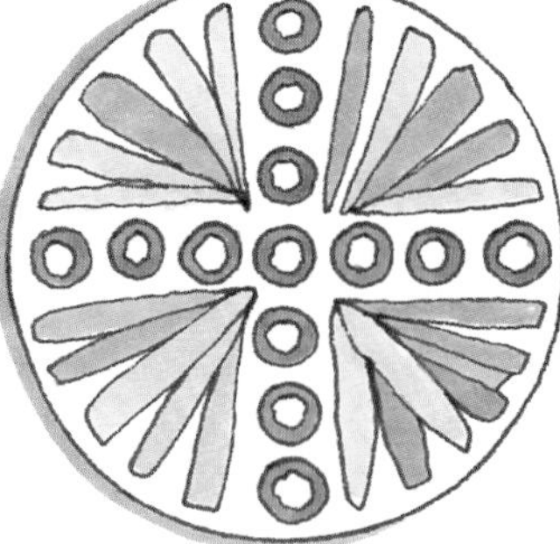

VEGETABLE DIP

Slice carrots, cucumbers, zucchini, and celery sticks into small, thin strips and serve with a dip. Avoid any strong or spicy ingredients. Try mixing honey with mustard or ketchup, relish, and mayonnaise.

Party CAKES

3 · CAKES

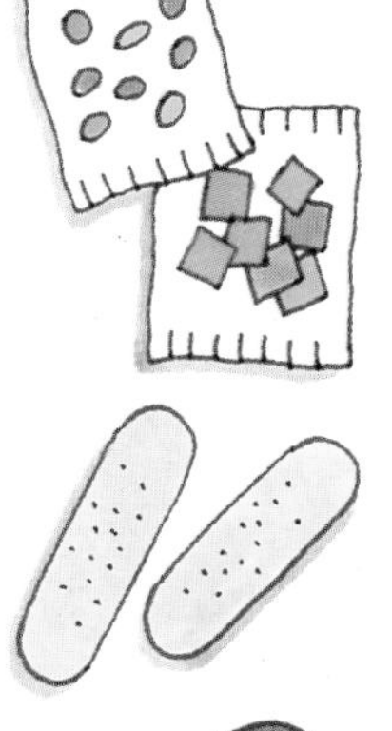

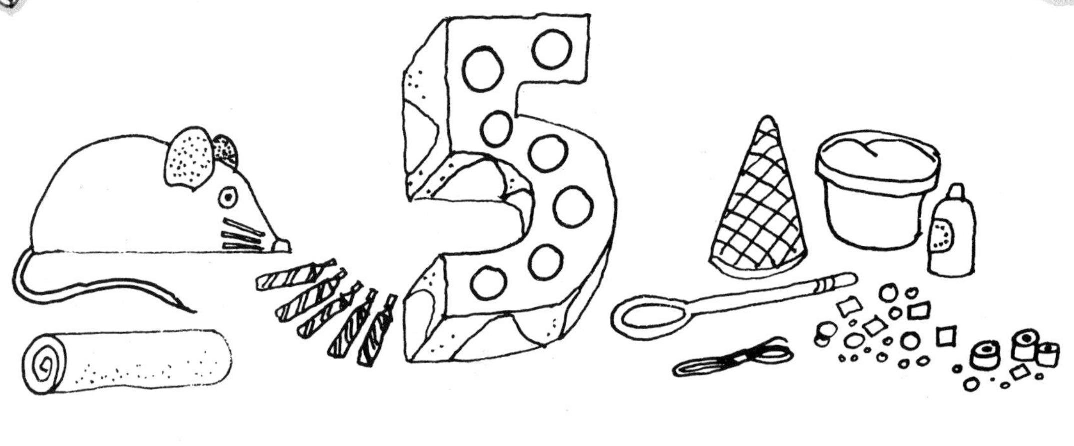

INTRODUCTION

If you are ever stuck for new ideas for children's party cakes - or are not sure how to make novelty cakes - then this section will help you. Everything here is explained in a straightforward way, and detailed pictures clearly explain each stage. Your children will love helping with the cooking and decorating, as well as eating the results!

The easy basic sponge cake recipe on page 52 shows you step-by-step how to create fun and attractive cakes - for birthdays or other special celebrations.

The instructions show you how to create several variations of each basic idea. Following the same methods, you might like to try experimenting with some of your own ideas.

There are plenty of tips on decorating your cakes too, using fondant or butter icing with simple added extras, such as wafers and candy. Always avoid using whole nuts and candy that could get stuck in small children's throats.

Many of the cakes can be linked to a party theme, for example, a space party or a circus party.

Ingredients are given in both imperial and metric measures. It is best to use either imperial or metric, but not a mixture of both.

Natural food colorings are available. When you go shopping, look at the alternatives and carefully check the ingredients. Buy those which don't contain sugar, preservatives, and artificial ingredients.

At the end of this section there are several additional ideas for you to try. It might be a good idea to keep a "Party file" of magazine cuttings for future use.

BASIC RECIPES

You will need...

2 x 8″ (20 cm) round cake pans
6 oz. (175 g) softened butter or margarine
6 oz. (175 g) super fine sugar
3 medium eggs
6 oz. (175 g) self-rising flour

1 Preheat oven to 350°F (180°C). Put the softened butter and sugar in a mixing bowl. Beat together with a wooden spoon until the mixture is pale and creamy. Add the beaten eggs to the mixture a little at a time, stirring well until it is smooth.

2 Sieve the flour into the mixture and fold in carefully until well mixed. The cake mixture should be soft and light. Grease pans with butter or margarine, add a little flour, shake, then empty out (or use a pastry brush and a teaspoon of oil). Pour half the cake mixture into each greased pan and smooth until level.

3 The cake is done when well-risen and brown. It should feel springy in the middle and be starting to shrink away from the edge of the pan. As an extra test, insert a warm metal skewer into the middle of the cake – if it comes out clean then the cake is ready. Turn onto wire racks to cool.

Variations

Chocolate – add a little hot water to 1 oz. (25 g) of cocoa and mix to a paste (or melt the same amount of chocolate). Beat into the creamed butter and sugar mixture.

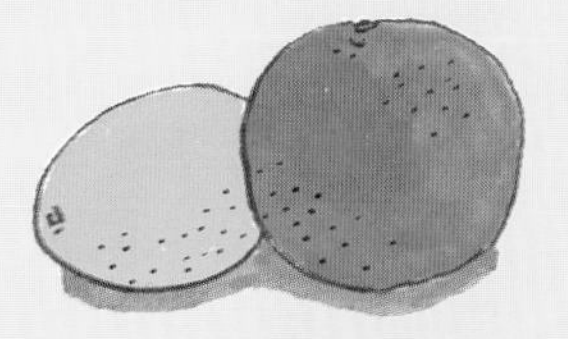

Orange or lemon – finely grate the rind of one orange or lemon and add to the cake mixture. For extra flavor add a little of the juice.

Marble – divide the creamed mixture in half. Add a little hot water to 1 oz. (25 g) of cocoa and mix to a paste. Mix into the creamed mixture. For different colors, add a few drops of food coloring and mix well. Place alternate spoonfuls of the two mixtures in pans.

Butter icing

Butter icing can be used to stick cakes together, and to make a rough surface decoration. Use half the amount of butter to the amount of confectioner's sugar (you can use margarine instead) i.e., 3 oz. (75 g) of butter to 6 oz. (175 g) of confectioner's sugar. Beat the confectioner's sugar into the bowl a little at a time, mixing in with the butter. If too thick to spread stir in a little milk. Use a piping bag to apply the icing or a warm knife to spread it. As a less sweet alternative, make an icing from soft cream cheese mixed with lemon or orange juice, and honey.

Fondant icing

Fondant icing is ideal for covering and modeling. Buy packets (in a baking or specialty store) of 8 oz. (225 g) or 16 oz. (450 g) and roll out to desired thickness. Cover rolling pin with confectioner's sugar first to prevent it from sticking to the icing. When covering cakes, apply a little jelly to the cake surface first to help it stick. Use your fingers to mold fondant icing and cover joints, with a little water if necessary. To cover a dome-shaped cake, roll out the icing into a circle and then mold it around the cake. Keep fondant icing covered when not using it to stop it from drying out.

Glacé icing

Glacé icing is very simple to make and covers cakes easily. Sift 6 oz. (175 g) of confectioner's sugar into a bowl. Add hot water a little at a time, mixing it with the sugar to make a smooth paste that is easy to spread.

Decoration

Cake decorations such as silver balls and plastic flowers, candy, and dried or fresh fruit can all be used. Avoid whole nuts as these can choke small children. Marzipan or fondant icing can be shaped into figures.

Press differently shaped objects into icing while it is still soft to form interesting patterns.

You can color icing or marzipan by adding a few drops of food coloring and kneading well, or by painting with a brush after modeling.

Press fondant icing through a garlic press to make "hair" and "branches."

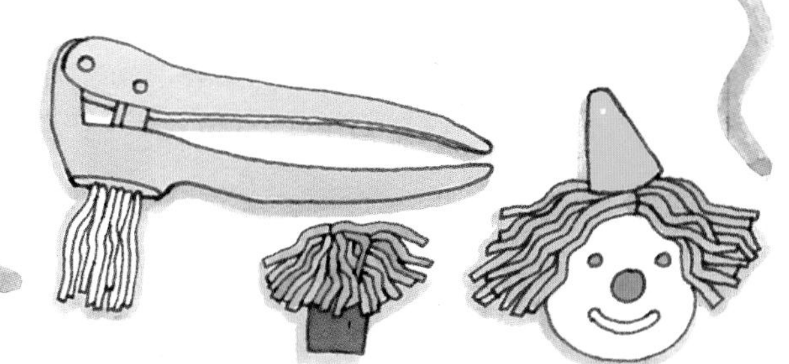

BASIC CAKES

You can create all kinds of novelty cakes by cutting and building with the basic shapes shown below. Stick the pieces together with butter icing.

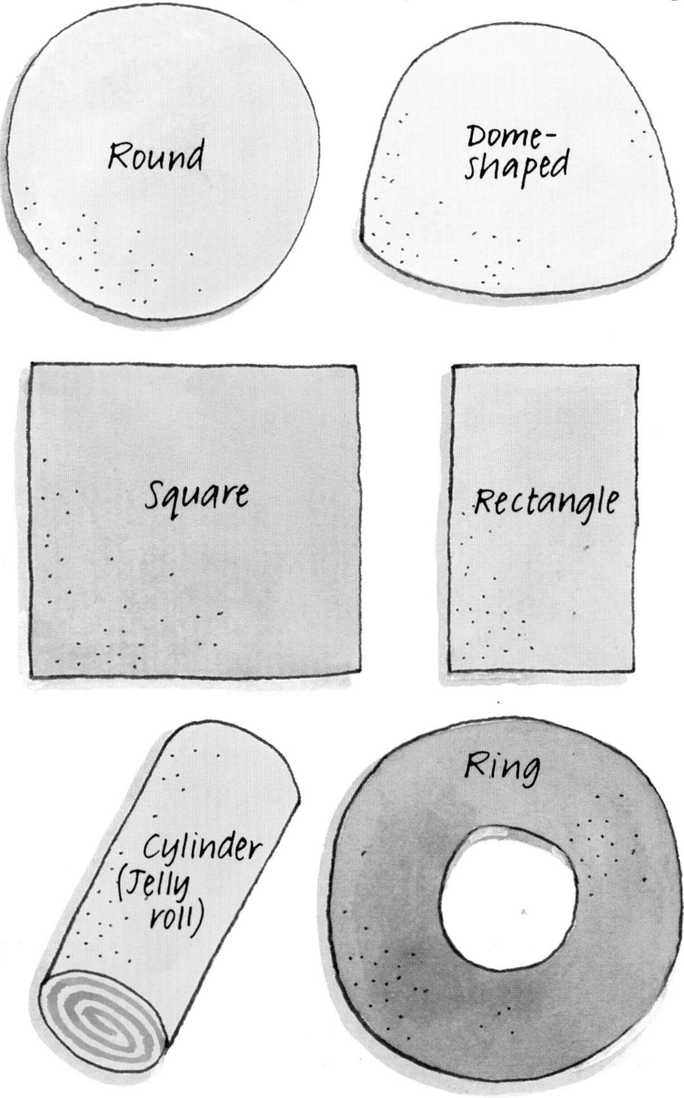

Small cakes, cookies, ice cream cones, and wafers are ideal for details such as ears and arms.

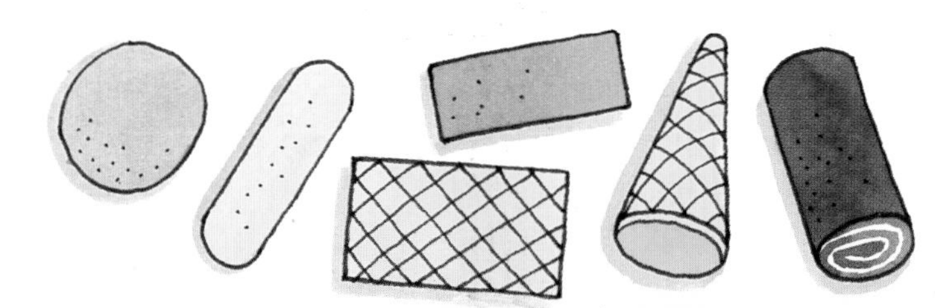

Here are two simple ideas from pieces joined together.

MONSTER CAKE

Cut a ring cake in two, slide alongside each other and stick together.

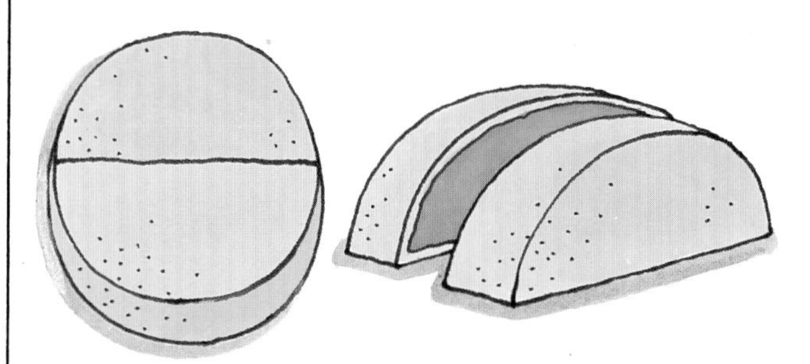

RAINBOW CAKE

Cut a round cake in two, stand up and stick together. You could cover the cake in fondant icing and paint stripes with a brush and food coloring, or apply butter icing using a knife or piping bag.

NUMBER CAKES

Hire, buy, or borrow the cake tins and use the same number of decorations on top.

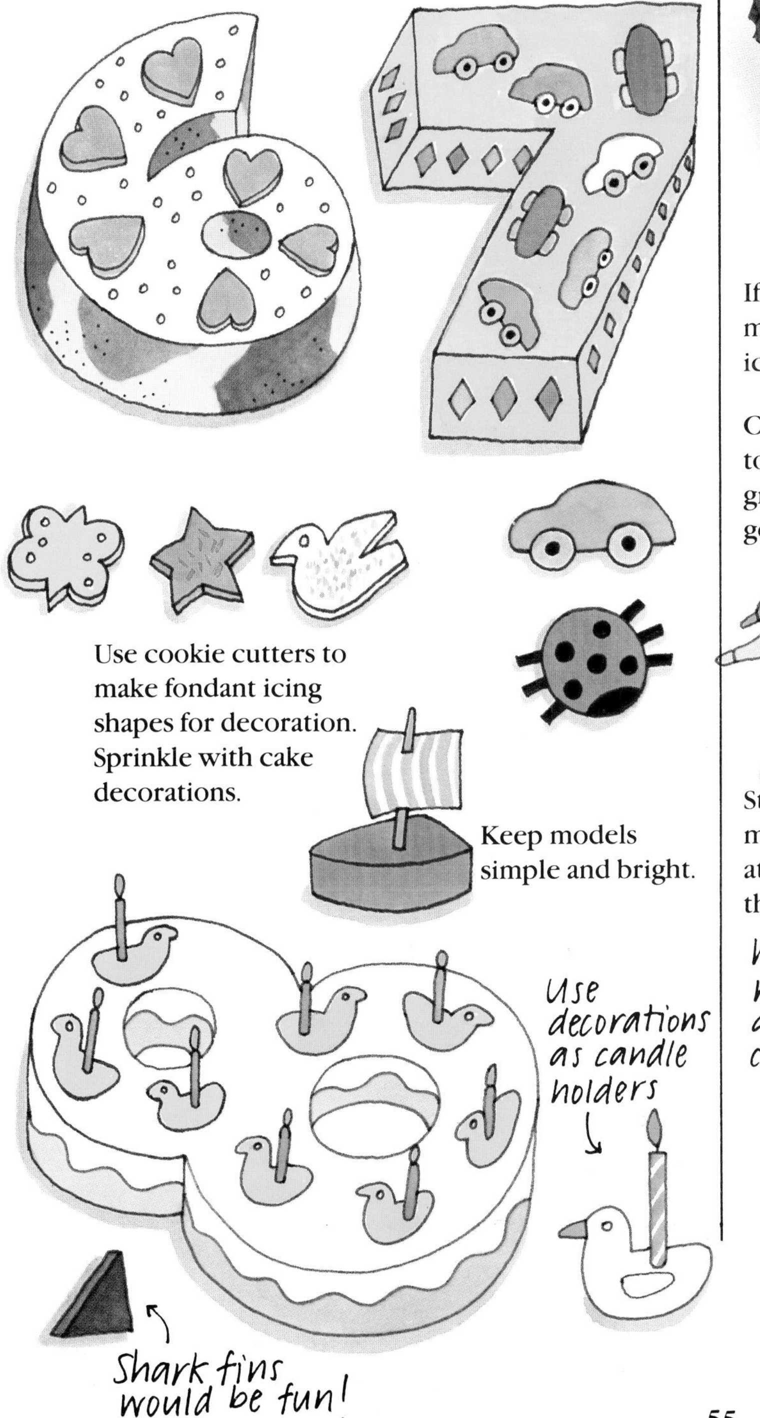

Use cookie cutters to make fondant icing shapes for decoration. Sprinkle with cake decorations.

Keep models simple and bright.

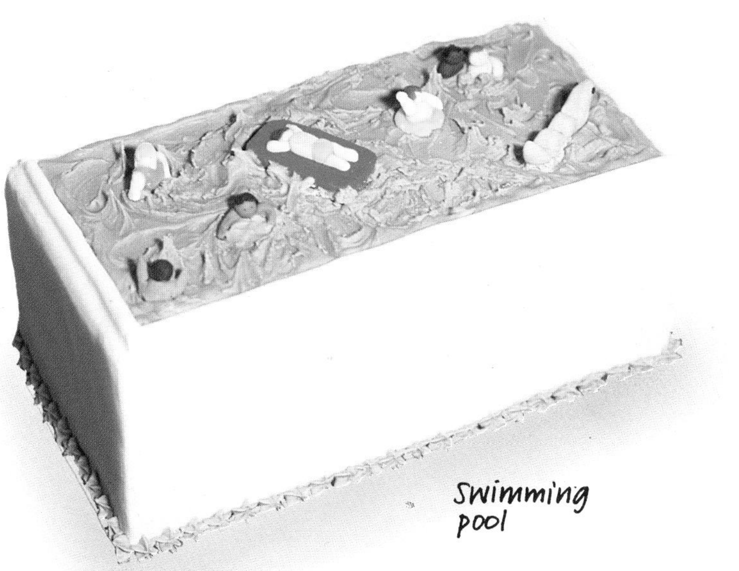

If you have a party with a theme, it can be fun making a cake to match. Cover a simple shape in icing and model figures.

Soccer cake

Chocolate logs topped with green icing make good trees.

Start making your models early, a few at a time, and keep them in a tin.

Write a message with a brush and food coloring

Ice-skating-cake

Happy Birthday

CLOWN

You will need...

1 small dome-shaped sponge cake
1 large dome-shaped sponge cake
16 oz. (450 g) fondant icing
2 "lady fingers"
1 ice cream cone
Food coloring
Candy

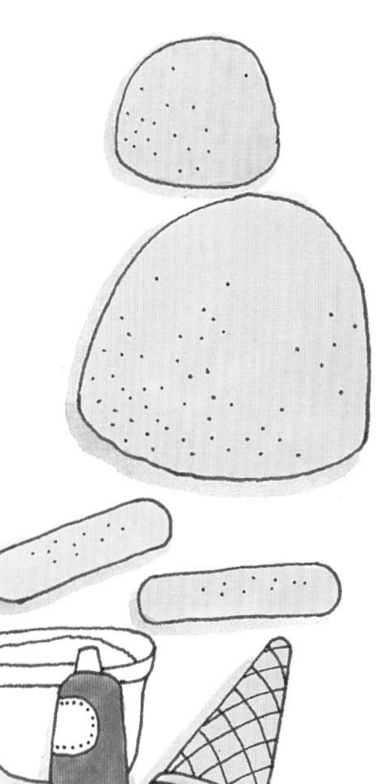

1 Color and roll out 11 oz. (300 g) of icing to cover the body and for sleeves. Roll out 4 oz. (100 g) of white icing and cover the head and "lady fingers." Press the head and arms into the body.

2 Decorate the clown's body by pressing candy into the icing. Use candy to make a nose and eyes. For mouth use a short strip of licorice.

3 Color the remaining fondant icing orange to make hair and cut into a fringe shape. Press carefully around the head. Cut the ice cream cone to fit the head and use as a hat.

WITCH/WIZARD

Use cookie cutters to make fondant icing shapes for decorations.

Make a banner from a strip of paper and two toothpicks.

Cover the clown's hat in fondant icing and decorate.

CASTLE

You will need...

3 x 7" (18 cm) square sponge cakes
4 jelly rolls
2 lb. (900 g) fondant icing
Food coloring
Licorice
Jelly or butter icing

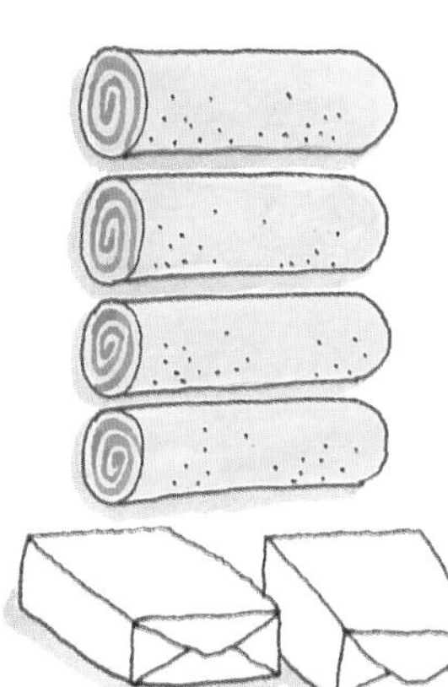

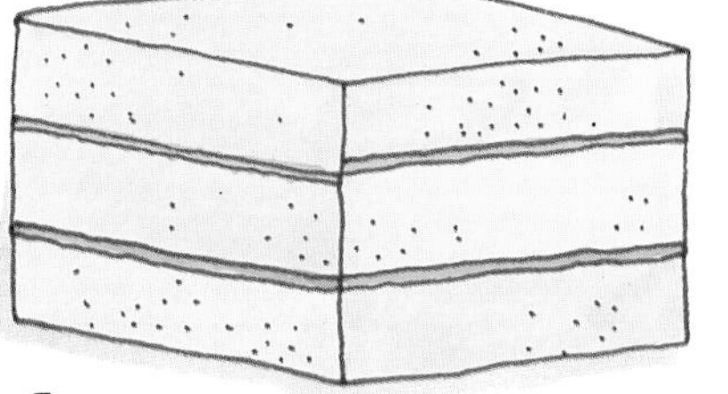

1 Assemble the cakes in layers with jelly or icing. Cut "bites" out of each corner. Add coloring to the icing, kneading well to mix. Roll out half of the icing and cover the cake.

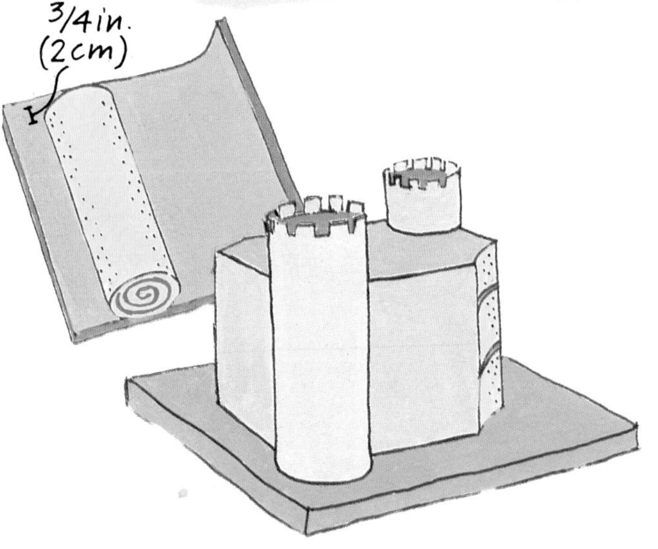

2 To make towers, roll out fondant icing to cover the jelly rolls, leaving ¾ in (2 cm) spare at the top. Cut out squares from this, then cover each roll and stick them to the castle with jelly or butter icing.

3 Cut licorice strips to make windows and a drawbridge, and stick them to the sides of the castle with jelly or icing.

For the finishing touch, make flags out of paper, stuck onto toothpicks.

FAIRYTALE CASTLE

Make this castle in the same way, placing icing- covered ice cream cones on top of the towers. Decorate the castle with bright cake decorations.

You could also add tiny toy knights.

RABBIT

You will need...

1 small dome-shaped sponge cake
1 large dome-shaped sponge cake
2 "lady fingers"
8 oz. (225 g) butter icing
Whipped cream
Brown or black food coloring
Licorice candy

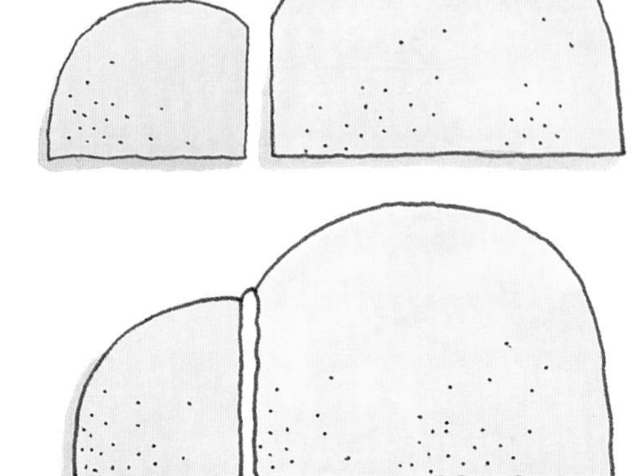

1 Cut a slice off one side of each cake and stick the cakes together using a little of the butter icing.

2 Divide the icing and color one batch. Use both batches to cover the body, using a knife or piping bag. Cover the "lady fingers" and press in place on the cake.

3 Make the rabbit's face from candy. Before serving, arrange a big blob of whipped cream for a tail.

For a birthday you could place candles in holders and stick them along the back of the cake. You could model a carrot out of marzipan or fondant icing and place it next to the rabbit for a good finishing touch.

TEDDY BEAR

You will need...

2 round sponge cakes
4 mini jelly rolls
8 oz. (225 g) butter icing
Small amount of
fondant icing
Yellow and red
food coloring
Candy

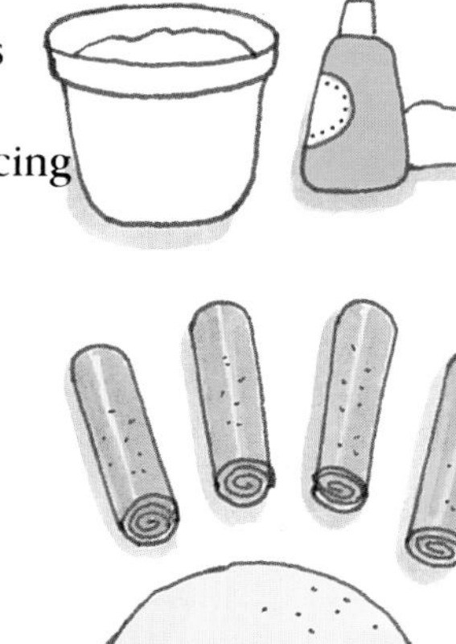

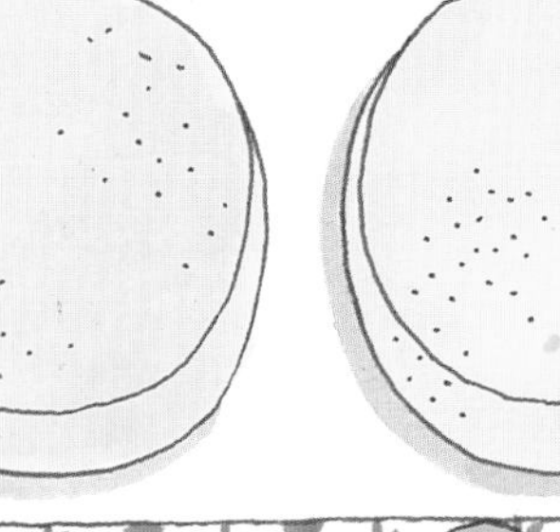

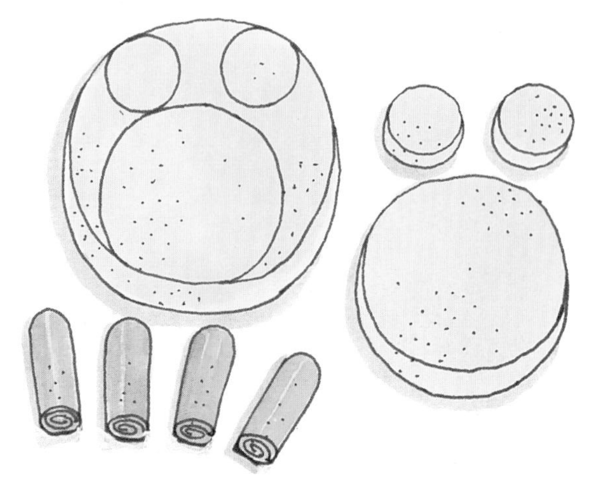

1 Cut one cake into a smaller circle for the head, and two little circles for the ears.

2 Assemble the teddy bear on a tray or board. Stick all the parts together with butter icing. Color the rest of the icing and cover the whole body, using a knife or piping bag.

3 Stick on candy or fondant icing to make eyes, nose, and mouth. Color the fondant icing, cut a bow tie out of it, and decorate with silver balls.

SUN
LADYBUG
PANDA
Use licorice to make antennae and spots
Surround cake with "lady fingers" and wafer cookies
Make like the teddy bear but cover in black and white fondant icing
Add candle "buttons" down the tummy

ROCKET

You will need...

1 jelly roll
1 ice cream cone
6 wafer cookies
16 oz. (450 g) fondant icing
Licorice candy
Blue food coloring
Small amount of glacé icing (optional)
Candles and hoiders (optional)

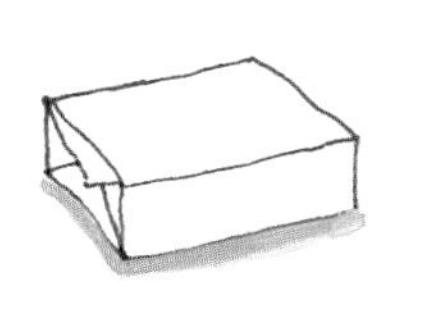

1 Divide the icing in half and add drops of coloring to one half, kneading well to mix. Roll out to about ⅛ in. (3 mm) thick. Roll out the rest of the icing.

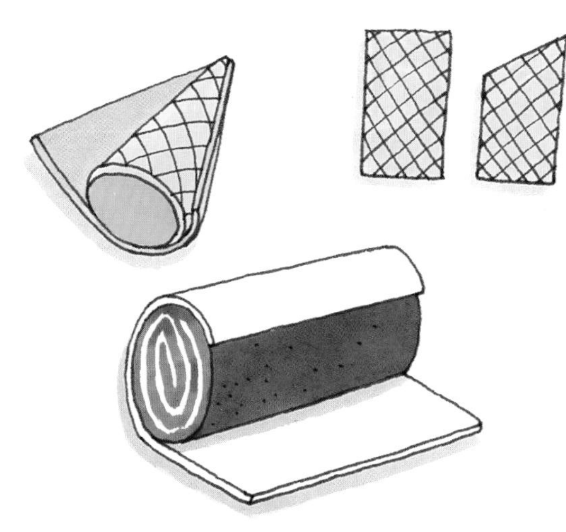

2 Carefully wrap the blue icing around the ice cream cone. Cut one corner off each wafer. Cover the jelly roll with white icing, pinching the edges to seal.

3 Assemble the rocket by standing the jelly roll on end on a plate or board. Push the wafers in evenly around the base. Place the cone on top and pinch icing together.

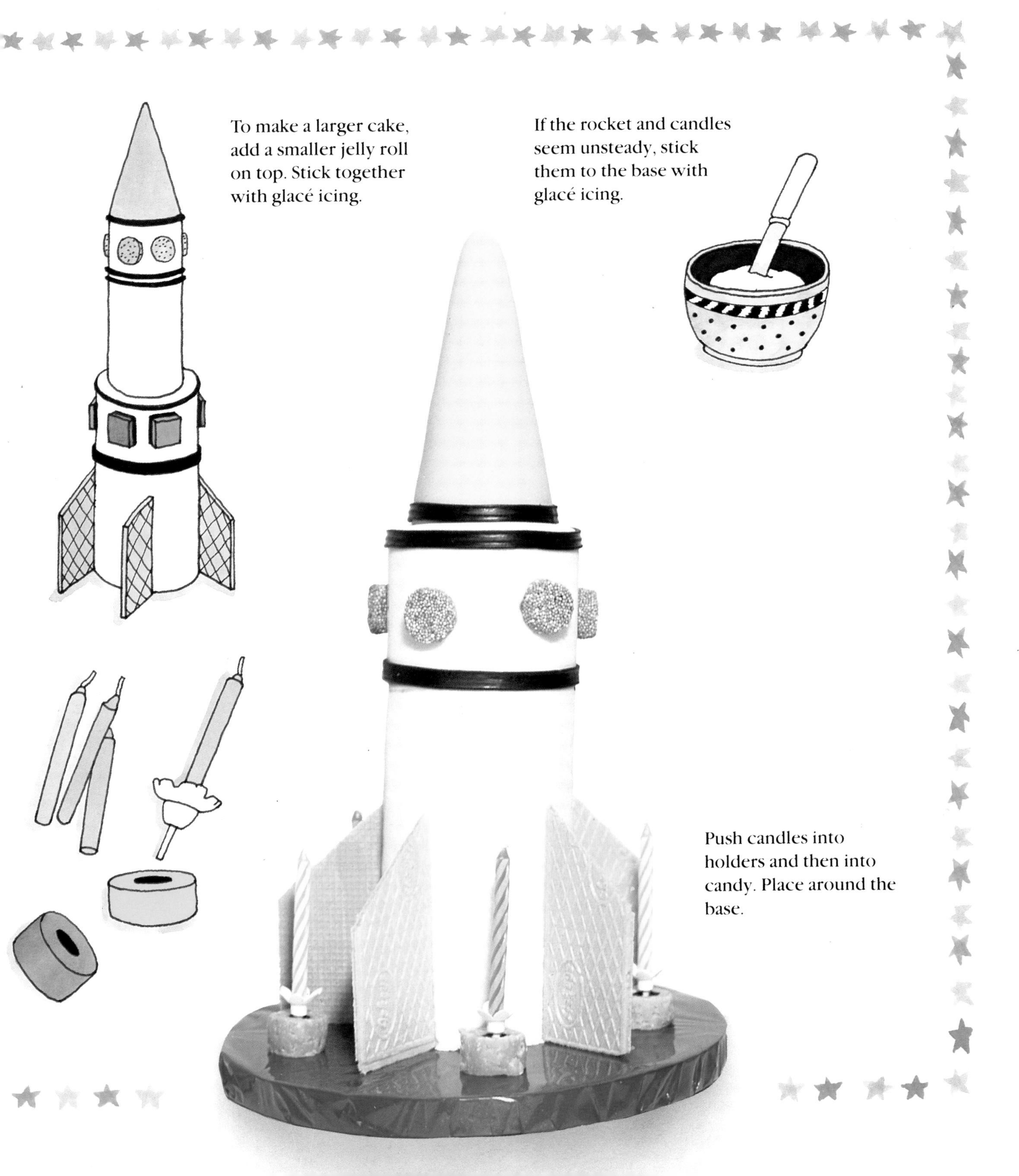

To make a larger cake, add a smaller jelly roll on top. Stick together with glacé icing.

If the rocket and candles seem unsteady, stick them to the base with glacé icing.

Push candles into holders and then into candy. Place around the base.

BUTTERFLY

You will need...

1 x 8″ (20 cm) round
marble sponge cake
16 oz. (450 g)
fondant icing
2 "lady fingers"
3 food colors
Candy, licorice, and
cake decorations

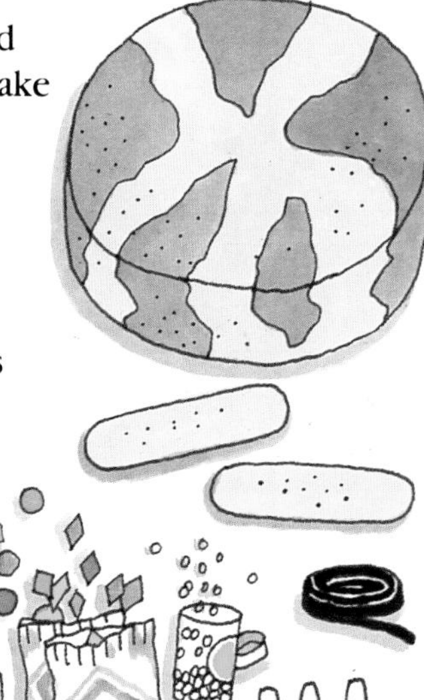

1 Cut the cake into two halves and put them back to back. Cut each "lady finger" to fit as the body of the butterfly.

2 Divide the icing into three equal parts and color each piece by kneading well with a few drops of food coloring. Roll out and cover the top of the cake and the "lady fingers."

3 Decorate the butterfly with candy and pretty cake decorations. Make the antennae from pieces of licorice.

BAT CAKE

You can add licorice "wing lines" if you like

Follow the same instructions as for the butterfly, using a marble sponge cake and "lady finger." Cut three "bites" out of the straight edge of each half of the cake. Place together, position body, and cover with black icing. Add icing ears and candy eyes.

DINOSAUR

You will need...

2 round sponge cakes
2 "lady fingers"
8 oz. (225 g) butter icing
3 wafer cookies
Candy
Food coloring

Sandwich two cakes together with butter icing

Cut the cake as shown. Use piece number 1 for the head, following through to number 7 for the tail

1 2 3 4 5 6 7

1 Cut up the cakes as shown above, arranging the pieces into a dinosaur shape on a board or tray. Stick them together with butter icing.

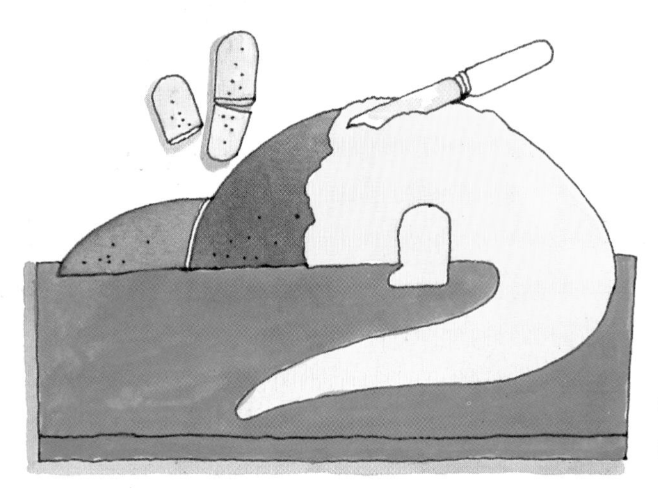

2 Liberally cover the whole dinosaur with butter icing. Cut the "lady fingers" in half and press into position as feet. Cover these with icing.

3 Cut the wafers into three triangular pieces and stick them along the top of the dinosaur. Decorate with candy, using two large pieces for the eyes.

Make tiny trees out of green fondant icing and chocolate logs.

Sharks, whales, and snowmen are all easy to model.

BUS

You will need...

2 2 lb (1 kg) sponge cakes
2 jelly rolls
16 oz. (450 g) fondant icing
Red and black food coloring
Candy
Jelly or butter icing

1 Make the bus body by cutting a quarter off one cake and sticking both cakes together with jelly or butter icing. Cut sections out of the jelly rolls as shown, and stick in position as wheels.

2 Color 11 oz. (300 g) of the icing red and roll out to cover the bus. Then cover 4 oz. (100 g) of icing black, roll out, and cover the wheels. From the remaining white icing, measure and cut a strip for the windows.

3 Stick candy on for hubcabs and headlights. With any remaining icing cut out passengers, paint them with food coloring, and press onto the windows.

TRUCK

By changing the shape of the top edge you can make different vehicles. For example, using a smaller piece of cake on top you can make a truck. Put small bags of candy or raisins on the back.

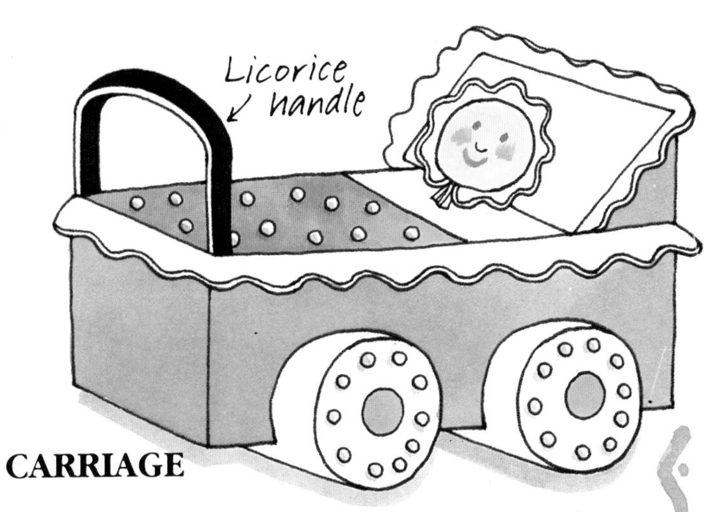

CARRIAGE

Making a carriage is just as easy. Decorate it with silver balls and strips of fondant icing pressed into frills.

MORE IDEAS

Here are three more cakes easily made and decorated.

CATERPILLAR CAKE

You will need about 4 jelly rolls for this cake.

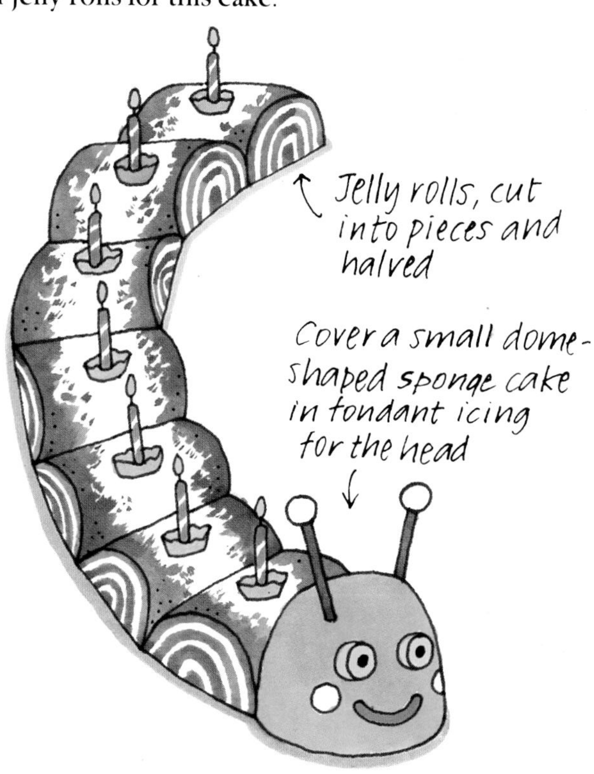

CHEESE AND MICE CAKE

Use two-quarters of a round sponge cake stuck together with jelly or butter icing.
Gently press "holes" into yellow fondant icing with the end of a wooden spoon.

TRAIN CAKE

Use mini jelly rolls to make this cake.

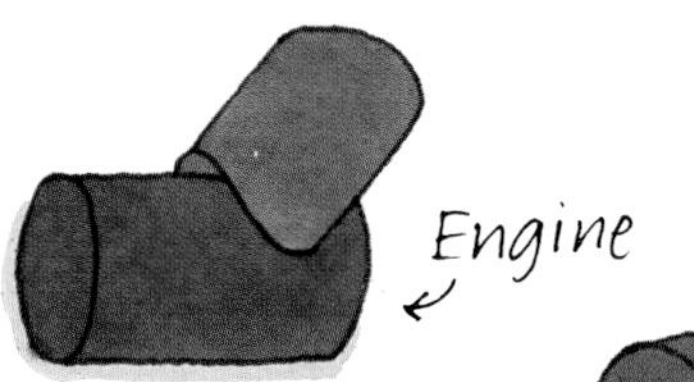

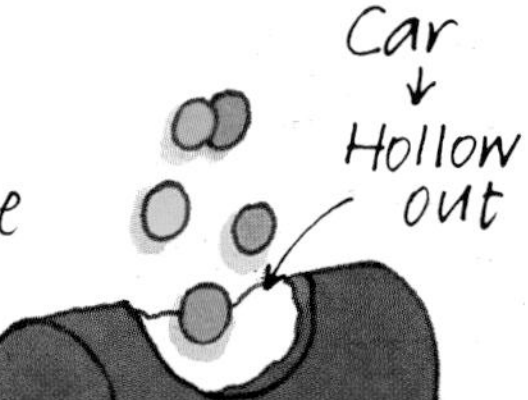

Party GAMES

4 · GAMES

INTRODUCTION

Games are perhaps the most essential element of any children's party. This section is full of all sorts of different games – some you will recognize as variations on traditional favorites, while others involve you and the children in making novel props for games based on a theme, such as a "black hole" for a space party.

Children need to release their energy running and jumping around, so there are plenty of races and musical games to choose from. Make sure you have enough space cleared indoors if you can't hold the party outdoors.

It's a good idea to intersperse these energetic games with quieter activities. You'll find the pencil and paper games and guessing games explained in this section to be popular. Children also enjoy making or drawing things, especially if they can then use them afterward in a game.

Some of the games are more suitable for younger children – some for older ones. Most can be adapted for any age group as the basic rules are very simple. Many of the games are more fun when played in teams, especially if the number of guests is large.

PREPARATION

Be well prepared before the day of the party. It's a good idea to enlist some extra adult help on the day to set up each game in advance, so you avoid delays between games when children may get restless. Keep an eye on the time; starting off the party with games, serving refreshments in the middle, then having time for more games afterward. If the weather permits, hold games outside for the space. If you are holding a party indoors, move furniture to the sides of your largest room, and move anything breakable.

VARIETY

Try and alternate energetic, noisy games with quieter ones. However, if a game is particularly enjoyed and doesn't require a lot of setting up, for example races or musical chairs, don't be worried about repeating it. It may be a good idea to have some "sitting down" games right after refreshments so the children don't feel sick rushing around!

PLAN

Make a list of all the games you intend playing, in the order you intend to play them. Then split the list into two – the first half for games to play before refreshments, and the other half for afterward. Always have more games planned than you think you will need as it's difficult to judge how long each one will take. It is a good idea to try out any new games beforehand to ensure they work.

GAMES TO PLAY
1. Jungle art
2. Spotted dog
3. Teddy bear pass
4. Black hole
5. Treasure hunt
6. Guessing game
7. Dares

RULES

Whatever games you play, keep the rules simple and explain them clearly at the beginning. Take into account the age and sex of the party guests when deciding on the games. Whatever you decide, little boys and girls can be very determined if they decide they don't want to play a certain game!

JOINING IN

You often find that there's one child who feels too shy at first to join in with the others. Get them involved by asking them to help set things up. Be careful about incorporating too many games where some people will have to "sit out", as some children may get upset or become bored.

MUSIC

Make sure you have some music organized for your party. Children love to dance and jump around to popular tunes, and many party games need music to play them properly. You can buy special party tapes for children, or you could make your own. Make someone in charge of the music.

PROPS

Have all your props together in a box – music tapes, small prizes, stopwatch, etc. You can make some of these beforehand with your child. Masks or buttons are simple to make, and you can suit them to a theme if you are having one.

PRIZES

Children enjoy winning prizes, but they don't need to be expensive. Toy shops are full of little novelties, such as miniature packs of cards and pads of stationery. Small boxes of crayons are also popular. Try to avoid giving out too much candy, especially before refreshments. "Pass the Package" is always a popular game to play. Rather than having just one prize in the center, you could place a few little ones between other layers.

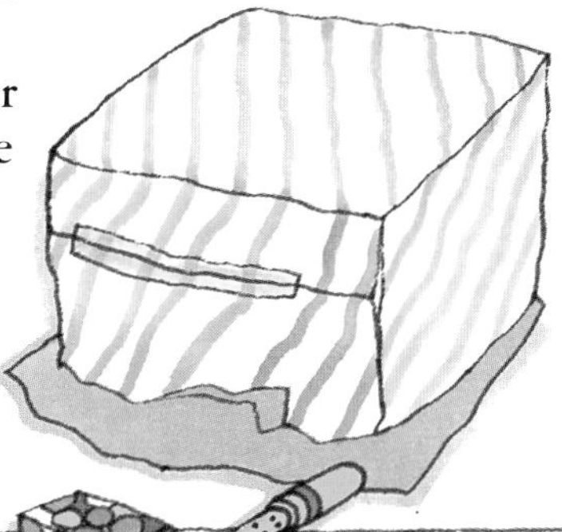

Buttons or small toys

Rather than just giving a prize to the winner of a game, have some games where a team, or everyone taking part, wins something. If you are giving out prizes, it might be a good idea to put them in the party favor bags so the children can easily find them later to take home.

Emma

RACES

Races are better held outdoors, though some can be held indoors if the room is big enough. Clear away as much furniture as possible to the sides of the room, and move anything breakable!

THREE-LEGGED

Divide the party guests into pairs and tie them together by the ankle (not too tightly) using old ties or rope.
Hold relay races in teams.

RED ROVER

The more players you have for "Red Rover" the better. Everyone lines up on one side of the room or yard. One person is chosen to stand alone, some distance from the line. When he or she shouts "Red Rover move over," everyone must run over to the other side while the caller tries to catch someone. Whoever is caught joins the caller as the others run back the other way. Together they try and catch more people. Whoever is the last to be caught is the winner.

EGG & SPOON

Don't play this messy game indoors!
Everyone lines up holding a spoon with an egg balanced in it. Whoever makes it to the finish line with their egg still intact on their spoon, wins.

WHEELBARROW

A wheelbarrow race is run in pairs. One person gets down on all fours, while their partner picks them up by their ankles. When everyone is ready in this position, they set off for the finish line - trying not to collapse!

SACK RACE

Potato sacks are the best to use for a sack race, though plastic garbage bags or old pillowcases are more easily available. Have a start and finish line. The best technique is to jump with both feet together, holding the sack with both hands!

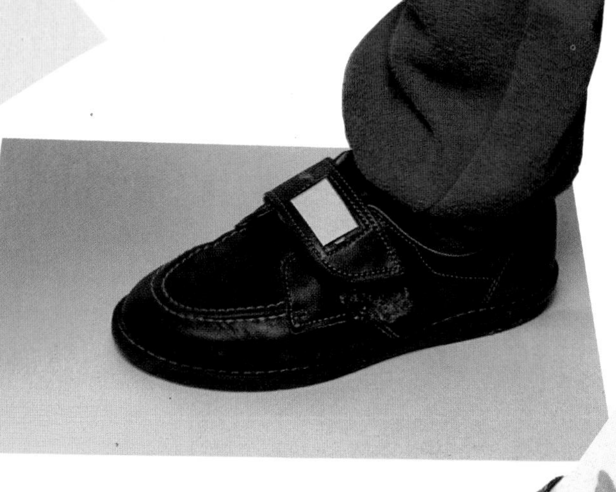

STEPPING STONES

Stepping stones is a simple but fun game. All you need are two sheets of paper per player. As each player steps forward, they must place a sheet of paper in front of their foot to step on to. Before they can step forward again they must lift up their back foot, pick up the piece of paper, and balance on one foot while placing the paper in front again. It's not as easy as it sounds, especially if you make it a team race!

MEDALS

The birthday child can help to make these medals to give to the winners of races and team relays.

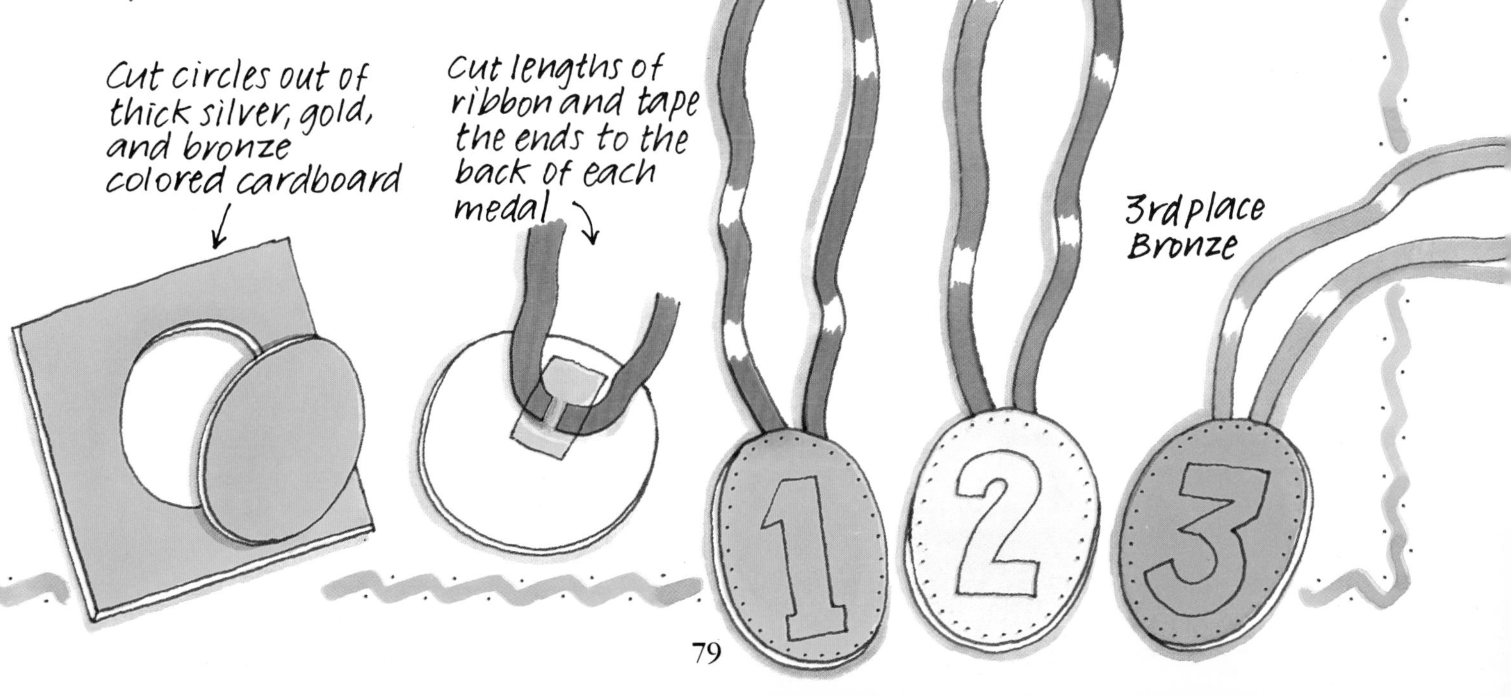

GUESSING

GUESS WHAT SMELL

Guessing games are always popular and make good competitions. To play "Guess What Smell" you will need a blindfold and a number of "smelly" items. Make some difficult, for example, a slice of bread, dish detergent - and some easy, for example, a rose or coffee. Each player has one guess per item, for which they get one point if it's correct. Whoever gets the most points is the winner.

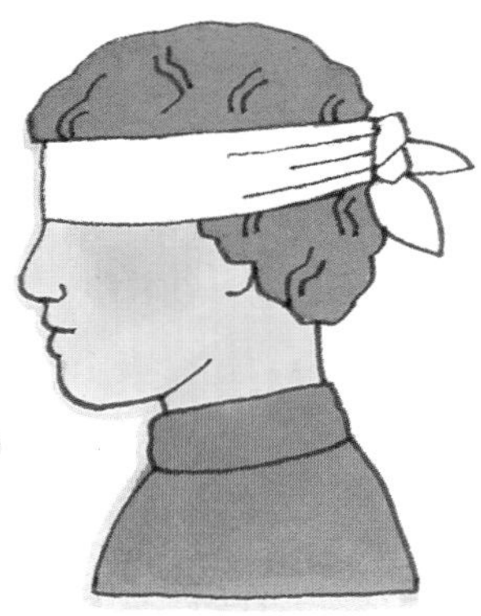

GUESS WHAT TASTE

The game is also played with a blindfold and involves guessing what things are by tasting them. Avoid too many strong tasting foods or players will feel sick! Try out sugar, salt, pudding, and cocoa. To make guessing more difficult, try various flavors of potato chips or jellies.

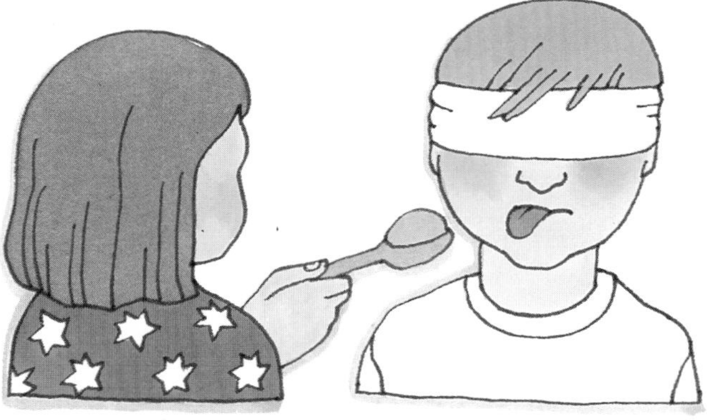

SQUEAK, PIGGY, SQUEAK

For this game, one person is blindfolded while the others sit around the room, preferably in soft chairs or on cushions. Whoever is blindfolded walks around the room and then sits down on someone's lap, saying, "Squeak, piggy, squeak." Whoever they are sitting on starts "squeaking," and the blindfolded person must try to guess the identity of the squeaker. If the guess is correct, the "squeaker" becomes the person to be blindfolded.

GUESS WHO

"Guess Who" is played in pairs. The organizer writes down the names of famous people or types of animals on bits of paper then pins one to the back of each player. One member of the pair then looks at the label on their partner's back and mimes that person or animal until the partner guesses who they are. They can't give spoken clues.

GUESS WHAT

You will need...

Cardboard box
Colored wrapping paper
Small household objects

Cover a cardboard box with colorful wrapping paper

Place the objects to be guessed inside

Cut out two holes in each side of the box, big enough for a child's hand to fit through

Players take turns to feel the objects in the box, writing down their guesses as they go along. You could set a time limit to make it harder. When everyone has had their turn, open the box and check the lists to find out who got the most guesses correct.

What objects you decide to put in the box will depend on the age group of the children at the party. Make most of them household items - some hard and some easy.

For younger children you could use a rubber duck, orange, toy car, comb, teddy bear, and sponge.

For older children you can have more difficult objects. For example, a hat, playing card, paper clips, banana, tube of toothpaste, pair of sunglasses, sandpaper, and a roll of tape.

PENCIL & PAPER

Party games tend to be noisy when there are lots of children, so it may be a good idea to include some quieter, less energetic games. This gives the organizers, and the guests, a rest! For most of the following games all you need to provide are pencils and paper.

LONG WORDS

To play this game you need to think of a long word, such as "nightingale." Players then have five minutes to write down all the words they can make out of "nightingale," for example, "night," "gale," "nail," "gate," etc. They must not be proper names. Count up the words. The winner is the person who has most words on their list.

LAST LETTERS

You can have any number of players for this game. Everyone sits in a circle. One person calls out the name of something. It can be a country, animal, vegetable, or a flower. If "daffodil" is called out, the other players must write it down and then try to think of a flower beginning with the last letter, for example, "lilac." Then a flower beginning with the letter "c," and so on until everyone gets stuck. Count up each player's list of words. The winner is the one with the most words. With older children, you could play this game without writing the words down, and just saying them out loud.

PICTURE WORDS

This is an amusing team game. Each person writes down the name of an object on a separate strip of paper, folds it up, and places it in a hat or bag. A member from one team picks out a piece of paper and looks at the word. He or she then has one minute to draw the word. The other team members must try to guess what the word is. If they guess the word before the time is up, the team wins a point. Each team should have the same number of turns, and the one with the most points at the end wins.

HEADS AND BODIES

"Heads and Bodies" is a drawing game which can produce hilarious results. Each player draws a hat at the top of a long piece of paper, and then folds it back along the bottom edge of the drawing. Everyone then hands their paper to the person on their left who draws a head and neck. Again, everyone folds the paper back, this time so that only the bottom of the neck can be seen, and passes it on. This continues for the body, the legs, and finally the feet. The papers are folded over for the last time and passed on. Unfold them for a surprise!

Fold over here

MEMORY GAME

Children love this memory test and it's guaranteed to keep them quiet! Before the party, lay out about a dozen objects on a tray, for example a hairbrush, button, candle, scissors, apple, and so on. When you are ready to play the memory game, carry the tray in to your guests. Tell them to look at it closely for one minute and memorize all the objects. Then take the tray away and hand out a pencil and paper to everyone. Give them a couple of minutes to write down everything they can remember. Whoever remembers the most, wins. You can make the "Memory Game" harder simply by adding extra items to the tray.

You will need...

Tray
Objects from around the house
Pencils
Paper

CLOWN TARGET

Children will enjoy helping to make these targets as well as playing the game. The clown's face shown here was created with a circus theme in mind, but you could make a spaceman's head for a space party, etc. This game is not recommended for younger children.

Fold here

Glue stick

Cut-out shapes

You will need...

Colored cardboard
Tissue paper
Scissors
Stick glue
Toothpicks
Adhesive putty
Large straws

1 Cut out a circle of cardboard for the clown's face and stick it onto one side of a folded rectangle of cardboard. Cut out shapes for the mouth, nose, and eyes and stick them onto the face.

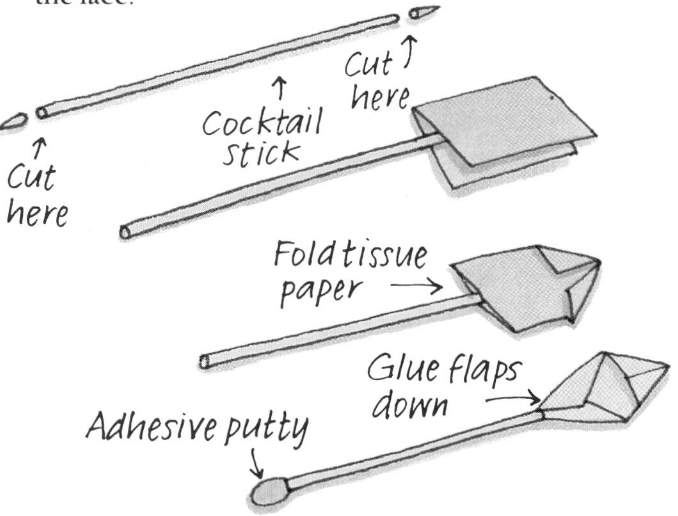

2 With a pencil, draw a line inside the mouth shape, leaving enough space to look like lips. Carefully cut out the rest of the mouth with a craft knife to leave a large hole.

3 To make the "arrows," cut the sharp ends off toothpicks. Then stick a small blob of adhesive putty on one end and a tissue paper diamond-shaped "tail" on the other end.

To fire...

Place the arrow, putty end first, down a straw, then blow hard down the straw, aiming to shoot the arrow through the clown's mouth.

Scoring

Make three arrows for each child and give points for direct hits. You could make a target for each child if numbers were small. Alternatively, make a couple of targets and hold competitions between teams.

WARNING:
Do **NOT** let children aim at each other

Ideas for other targets

Younger children could flip tiddlywinks into the clown's mouth, or throw candy from a marked distance.

CLOWN BALLOONS

Get the children to decorate balloons with clowns' faces. Draw a face using markers or cut out shapes for eyes, nose, and mouth from paper and stick onto a blown-up balloon. A good balloon game involves everyone standing in a line and passing the balloon, without using their hands, from one end of the line to the other. Play the game in teams. If someone drops the balloon it must go back to the beginning of the line again.

You could decorate balloons to suit other party themes

TREASURE HUNT

Treasure hunts are always popular with children, but you do need to prepare well before the party. Outdoors is the best place to hold a treasure hunt, especially if there are lots of participants, although clues could also be hidden indoors if there is enough space. Dividing the children into teams is more fun and more successful than playing individually.

You will need...

Pencil
Paper
Envelopes
"Treasure"

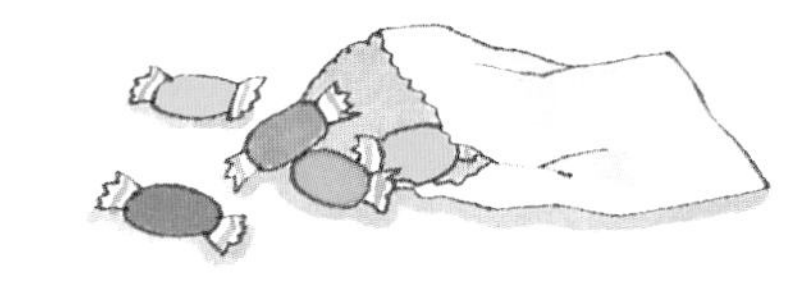

Depending on the number of children playing, divide them into at least two teams - Team 1, Team 2, etc. The organizer then works out approximately ten different hiding places for clues. For example, if the hiding place is under a wheelbarrow, the clue could say "The next hiding place is under something used for wheeling things around the garden."

Differently-colored envelopes for each team

There should be a copy of each clue for every team. The last clue should lead the teams to the treasure, which the organizer hides before the start of the game. The treasure could be candy or little toys. If you are having a theme party you could hide something appropriate, for example, chocolate coins at a pirate party.

Put each clue in a different envelope marked with the number of each team, and leave them in the hiding places, apart from the first clue which should be handed out at the start. To avoid one team just following another to each hiding place, try and place team's clues in a different order. The winning team is the one that finds the "treasure" first.

HUNT THE PUZZLE

Old birthday card

Cut into several large pieces

Cut up old birthday or Christmas cards to make puzzles, one for each child or team. You stick pictures from magazines onto thin cardboard and cut up. Strong, clear images work best. Hide the pieces separately around the house. The winner is the one who completes their puzzle first.

NATURE HUNT

A nature hunt is a good idea if you can play in a yard. Give each child a list of things to find, some easy, some more difficult. Here are some ideas:

Twigs
Leaves (various)
Stone
Feather
Seeds
Flower (various)

FIND THE BURIED TREASURE

Younger children may find clues hard to follow, so you could try this buried treasure hunt instead:

You will need...

Paints or pens
Papers
Scissors
Thin plastic sheet
Toothpicks
"Treasure"

Draw a tropical island scene on a large piece of paper. Then cut around the island, leaving the top edge uncut so that it can be lifted up. Place the paper over plastic and without the children seeing, mark an "X" on the plastic under the island. Each child must guess where the treasure is buried on the island by sticking in a flag (made from a toothpick and paper). Lift the island up to see whose flag is nearest the "X". The winner is awarded the treasure.

FAIRY DARES

This "daring" game can be adapted to any party with a theme. This version has a fairy theme, so instructions are given to show you how to make a wand pointer board and lily pads with different dares written on the back. The rules are simple – each child sits on his or her own lily pad in a circle and takes turns in spinning the pointer. Whoever it points to when it stops has to turn over their lily pad and perform the dare. When they have finished they can sit out. The last person left in is the winner.

Dare suggestions:

- You have been turned into a frog – jump up and down 10 times.
- Run around the circle singing, "Row, Row, Row Your Boat."
- Pat your head with one hand and rub your stomach with your other hand at the same time.

Wand pointer

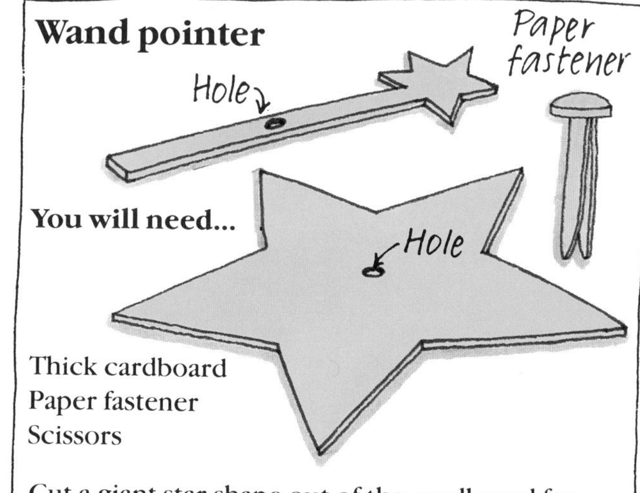

You will need...

Thick cardboard
Paper fastener
Scissors

Cut a giant star shape out of the cardboard for the board. Then cut out a smaller star and a long strip (for the shaft of the wand). Make a hole in the middle of the wand and the star. Place a paper fastener through the holes, flattening out the prongs at the back. Don't secure it too tightly or the wand won't spin.

Lily pads

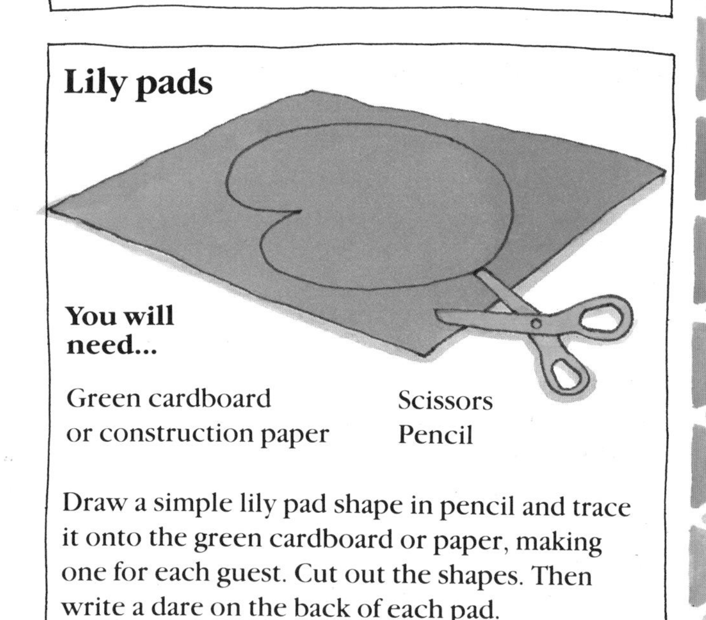

You will need...

Green cardboard or construction paper
Scissors
Pencil

Draw a simple lily pad shape in pencil and trace it onto the green cardboard or paper, making one for each guest. Cut out the shapes. Then write a dare on the back of each pad.

SPOTTED DOG

You will need...

Large piece of paper
Lots of small circles of black paper or "spot" stickers
Pen or pencil
Adhesive putty

For this game, you need to draw the basic outline of a dog and pin it to a wall. Divide the dog's body into areas, each scoring different points. Then stick a blob of adhesive putty to one side of the small circles of black paper. Each child is blindfolded and when it is their turn they are given several spots which they try to stick on the dog. If they miss altogether they get no points. At the end of each round add up the points to see who has scored the most.

MUSICAL SPOTS

With a "spotted" theme in mind, try "musical spots" as a variation on musical chairs.

You will need...

Cardboard or construction paper
Pen or pencil
Round object
Music

Use a large circular object to draw around on your cardboard or paper. Cut out one "spot" for each guest and place them in the center of the room. Play some music so the children can dance around the spots. When it stops they must sit down on a spot or they are out. Remove one spot each round. Whoever sits on the last spot has won.

MONSTER PLAY

Children love to make things, so why not let their imaginations run wild making a monster! You could divide the children into teams and hold a competition to see who can make the best monster. It might be a good way to start a party by getting everyone involved. Start collecting suitable materials well in advance. The following items would make good basics which you can add to depending on what you have around the house.

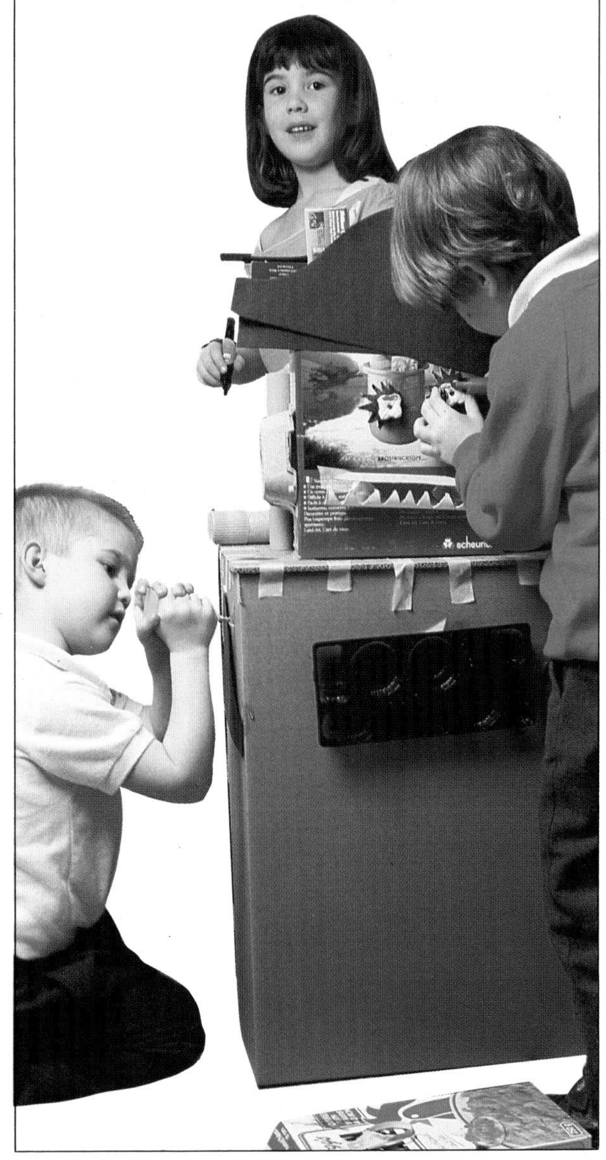

This is an activity that could be adapted to other party themes. For example, you could get the children to make an astronaut or a rocket at a space party.

MONSTER STATUES

For this game, children simply move around the room "monster-fashion" to music, making suitable monster noises! When the music stops they must hold whatever position they are in for several seconds until the music starts again. Anyone who moves has to sit out. This is a game that could be adapted to other themes. At a jungle party, each child could pick an animal to imitate.

WHAT'S THE TIME, MIGHTY MONSTER?

Replace the traditional "Mr. Wolf" character of this game with an equally menacing "Mighty Monster." The more players you have, the more fun the game is. Whoever is chosen as "Mighty Monster" starts walking away from the rest of the players, who then start following him or her. Everyone together asks loudly, "What's the time, Mighty Monster?" The "monster" can say any time it likes, but when the answer is, "12 o'clock, dinner time," everyone must run back to the starting place. "Mighty Monster" runs after them and whoever is caught, or is last home, becomes the next "Mighty Monster."

JUNGLE ART

Children love being able to create their own pictures, especially on a giant scale. Friezes and collages are often a good way of starting a party by getting the children involved from the moment they arrive. Some won't want to tear themselves away!

You will need...

Rolls of old wallpaper
Magazines
Colored construction paper
Pens or crayons
Scissors and glue
Tape or push pins

You don't have to be an artist to start off a frieze. Just pin or tape wallpaper to the walls in strips and draw very basic outlines. The children will do the rest.

For a collage, it may be a good idea to cut out some shapes ready for sticking and coloring in, or for drawing around.

Children will enjoy drawing around each other posing in different positions. Make sure they don't draw too close to the person or it will mark their clothes.

TEDDY BEAR PASS

To play "Teddy Bear Pass," the children must stand in a circle. Start playing some music and give a teddy bear to one child. He or she then passes it to their left and so on around the circle, from person to person. When the music stops, whoever is holding the teddy bear is out. The last person left holding the teddy bear is the winner.

TEDDY BEAR TEAMS

"Teddy Bear Teams" is a more difficult version of "Teddy Bear Pass," involving more skill and more teddy bears! The children divide into two teams and stand in a line. Someone says, "Ready, teddy, go!" and they start trying to pass a number of bears down the line using any part of their bodies except their hands. If a teddy bear touches the ground at all, it must go back to the beginning of the line again. Whichever team first manages to get all their teddy bears safely to the end of their line, wins a prize.

BLACK HOLE

Combining luck and skill, this game is a space variation of the traditional indoor fishing game using fishing rods and magnets.

You will need...

Colored paper (silver and gold)
Paper clips
Scissors
Tape
Magnet
String and pole
or stick
Garbage can or bucket
Black plastic garbage bag

1 To create a "black hole," line a bucket or garbage can with a black plastic garbage bag. You could decorate the outside by sticking on cut-out stars, planets, and rockets.

2 Using the colored paper, cut out stars, moons, planets, spacemen, and "alien" shapes. Instead of using silver paper, you could cover shapes with tinfoil.

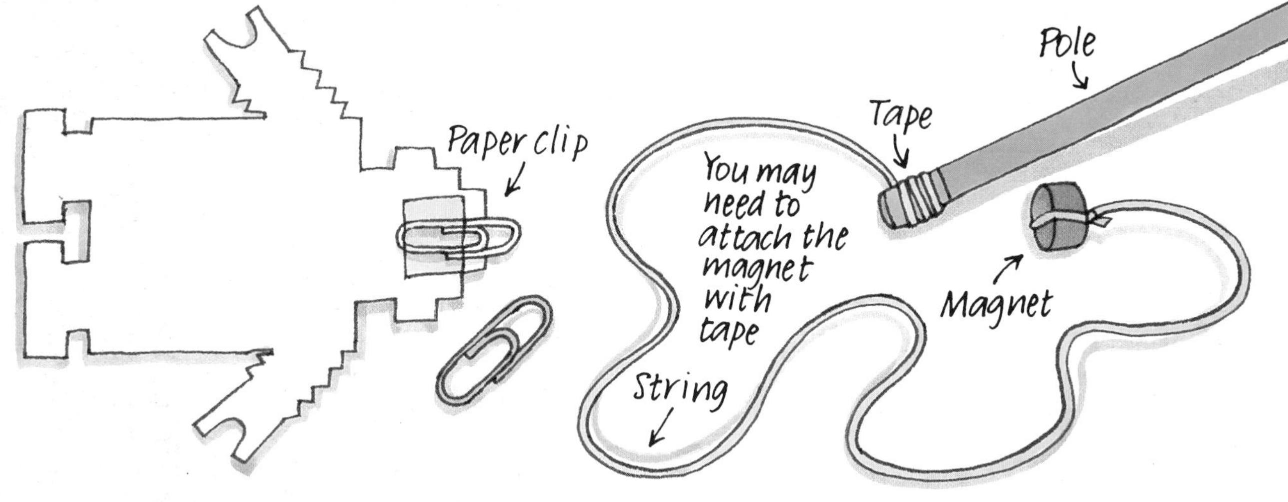

3 Attach a metal paper clip to the back of each shape using tape, leaving enough metal exposed to attract the magnet. Place the shapes at the bottom of the "black hole."

4 To make the "fishing rod," tie a piece of string to one end of a length of a pole or stick, securing it with tape. Then tie a small magnet to the other end of the string.

VARIATIONS:

You could paint a cut-down cardboard box to make a chest

Tape paper clips to chocolate coins and paper parrots

Pirate

Use a basket or a wooden chest as a container. "Fish" for chocolate coins and paper parrots.

Jungle

Decorate a cardboard box with green paper leaves and "fish" for paper animals.

Paper leaves

Cardboard box

How to play...

You could hold team competitions, writing different points on the back of the different shapes to be "fished" for. At the end of a time limit, add up each team's points to find the winners.

SILLY GAMES

There are some games that can only be described as "silly," but children often find them the most fun!

SWINGING APPLES

This game is a race to see who can eat their apple the quickest. Use a metal skewer to make a hole through the center of each apple. Then push a length of string through the hole and tie a knot. Hang the apples at mouth height, then munch away!

CANDY BOBBING

This game will be very messy, so make sure you put down newspaper or an old sheet if playing it indoors. Put some candy, such as marshmallows (avoid hard varieties that could choke children), on top of some flour or confectioner's sugar in a bowl. The players take turns to kneel down and try to pick the candy up without using their hands. Whoever manages to eat the most wins.

KINGFISHER BOOKS
Grisewood & Dempsey Inc.
95 Madison Avenue
New York, New York 10016

First American Edition 1992
10 9 8 7 6 5 4 3

Produced by Times Four Publishing Ltd.
Art and editorial direction: Tony Potter
Project editor: Regina Roselli Coles

Copy editor: Nicola Wright
Home economists: Nicola Bereen & Lycross Caterers

Library of Congress Cataloging-in-Publication Data
Beaton, Clare.
The complete book of children's parties/
Clare Beaton. – 1st American ed.
p. cm.
1. Children's parties – Juvenile literature. I. Title.
GV1205.B43 1992
793.2'1 – dc20 92-53104 CIP AC

ISBN 1-85697-807-9

Printed in Spain

    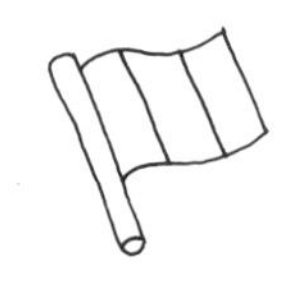